PARABOLA

THE MAGAZINE OF MYTH AND TRADITION

VOLUME XVI, NUMBER 3,
AUGUST, 1991

CRAFT

PARABOLA (ISSN: 0362-1596) is published quarterly by the Society for the Study of Myth and Tradition, Inc., a not-for-profit organization. Contributions are tax-deductible.

Subscription Rates: Single issue: $6.00. By subscription: $22.00 yearly, $38.00 for two years, $54.00 for three years. Postage for outside territorial U.S.: add $6.00 for surface rates, $20.00 for air, per year. **Postmaster:** Send address changes to PARABOLA, 656 Broadway, New York, NY 10012-2317. Second class postage paid at New York, N.Y., and additional offices.

Address all correspondence regarding subscriptions and advertising to Parabola, 656 Broadway, New York, NY 10012; Tel: (212) 505-6200; Fax: (212) 979-7325. Correspondence regarding editorial matters ONLY should be sent to The Editors, Parabola, 369 Ashford Ave., Dobbs Ferry, NY 10522; Tel: (914) 693-7960; Fax: (914) 693-7978. Parabola assumes no responsibility for unsolicited material. Manuscripts or artwork not accompanied by stamped, self-addressed envelopes will not be returned.

Distributed in the United States and Canada by Eastern News, 1130 Cleveland Road, Sandusky, Ohio 44870. Other foreign distribution is handled by PIMS, 105 Madison Avenue, New York, NY 10016.

Microform copies of Parabola may be obtained from University Microfilms, Inc. Parabola is indexed in the *Religion Index of Periodicals, Abstracts of English Studies, Book Review Index, Current Contents, Humanities Index, American Humanities Index,* and *CERDIC.*

VOLUME XVI, No. 3, AUGUST 1991

FOCUS

It is a very old belief (and who is to say that it has entirely disappeared, or that it is entirely mistaken?) that the process of creation is evolutionary growth: the bringing to perfection of all that is created, including matter and including man. God's intention, in other words, and the obedient tendency of nature, is toward "maturity," or perfection. In ancient times, metal ores were thought to be embryos of metals that would in time become gold, which (as the makers of the Tabernacle knew) is the most perfect of all metals, the metal of immortality and of the Sun. "Lead and other metals would become gold if they had time," says Subtle in Ben Jonson's play *The Alchemist.* Left to themselves, in the course of countless thousands of years, ores would grow into metals, and metals into gold; but with fire the metal worker could accomplish in hours what would take nature so many centuries; he could "transform" ores by smelting and change the character of metals. And by so doing, he himself was changed and took on the character of one set apart: a magician, a wielder of power, a collaborator with the Creator. In recognition of this, corresponding qualities were expected of him, and he had to obey certain disciplines. The alchemist, in Mircea

COVER: The Shoemaker. Sixteenth-century woodcut by Jost Amman.

Eliade's words, "must be healthy, humble, patient, chaste; his mind must be free and in harmony with his work; he must be intelligent and scholarly, he must work, meditate, pray . . ."

The gold of alchemy was just this hastened perfection, inner and outer, the divinization of matter and of man. This idea is certainly not strange to any craftsman. "When a man undertakes to create something," wrote Paracelsus, "he establishes a new heaven, as it were, and from it the work that he desires to create flows into him." In order that it may be expressed, that it may resound, the Word must be made flesh; immortality must be incarnated outwardly in gold and inwardly in the development of a subtle body within this ordinary body: the "glorious body," or "diamond body" of oriental tradition, the "spiritual body" of the Christian.

This "becoming" is what alchemy is about. Its process can also be expressed by the traditional formulas of initiation: the suffering, death, and resurrection of the god or the neophyte, represented by the substances in the crucible or by the material of the craftsman—the symbolic formula of transformation. Whether raw material, base metal, divine or human spirit, there must be the suffering of purification and separation. The patience that is the quality most vital to the craftsman is, in the final analysis, no other than this suffering, as it applies to the process of creation operating in and upon the artisan himself [Latin *patiens*, from *pati*, to suffer]. And as the alchemical substance is "punished," so is the craftsman's material: clay is pounded; flax beaten; wool teased, carded, and twisted; metal softened and struck. The substance, whether material or human, must change its character, be torn into separate elements in order to be reformed into something other—it must "die" in order to be "reborn."

And here we come to the central tenet of alchemy: its chief absurdity, proof (some would say) that in its operational sense at least it was all superstition and quackery; the idea that matter is alive. Yet, strangely enough, this is something that all craftsmen know to be true. They know that their material has a life of its own, a history, a character, needs, and possibilities unlike any other. They know that they must feel and understand this life so that a relationship can appear between it and their own. They accept a pattern for their work that is not theirs, that comes to them, as it were, from above; but their work is not merely to obey and to imitate, nor even only to "speed the process of nature," but to bring something peculiarly their own, some element of themselves, to unite with that other living entity, the material between their hands. Otherwise the relation does not exist; the material is indeed dead, and they themselves no more than copyists. The gold of the alchemist was not the same as natural gold; it was "living" gold. He added something even to the noblest of metals by his active relation with it.

The craftsman, as well as the alchemist, knows that his central task is the creation of himself; and it is above all for this aim that he strives with endless patience—as it is said in the Emerald Tablets of Trismegistus, separating "the subtle from the gross, softly and with great care," to make what his hands touch turn to gold. •

—*D.M. Dooling*

Adapted from "The Alchemy of Craft" in *A Way of Working*, D.M. Dooling, ed. (New York: Parabola Books, 1986).

PARABOLA
FALL 1991

The Use of Art

Ananda K. Coomaraswamy

In our traditional view of art, in folk-art, Christian and Oriental art, there is no essential distinction of a fine and useless art from a utilitarian craftsmanship. There is no distinction in principle of orator from carpenter, but only a distinction of things well and truly made from things not so made, and of what is beautiful from what is ugly in terms of formality and informality. The basic error in what we have called the illusion of culture is the assumption that art is something to be done by a special kind of man, and particularly that kind of man whom we call a genius. In direct opposition to this is the normal and humane view that art is simply the right way of making things, whether symphonies or airplanes.

Manufacture is for use and not for profit. The artist is not a special kind of man, but every man who is not an artist in some field, every man without a vocation, is an idler. The kind of artist that a man should be, carpenter, painter, lawyer, farmer, or priest, is determined by his own nature, in other words by his nativity. No man has a right to any social status who is not an artist.

We are thus introduced at the outset to the problem of the use of art and the worth of the artist to a serious society. This use is in general the good of man, the good of society, and in particular the occasional good of an

individual requirement. All of these goods correspond to the desires of men: so that what is actually made in a given society is a key to the governing conception of the purpose of life in that society, which can be judged by its works in that sense, and better than in any other way. There can be no doubt about the purpose of art in a traditional society: when it has been decided that such and such a thing should be made, it is *by art* that it can be properly made. There can be no good use without art: that is, no good use if things are not properly made. The artist is producing a utility, something to be used. Mere pleasure is not a use from this point of view.

MAN'S ACTIVITY consists in either a making or a doing. Both of these aspects of the active life depend for their correction upon the contemplative life. The making of things is governed by art, the doing of things by prudence. An absolute distinction of art from prudence is made for purposes of logical understanding, but while we make this distinction, we must not forget that the man is a whole man, and cannot be justified as such merely by what he makes; the artist works "by art and *willingly*."[1] Even supposing that he avoids artistic sin, it is still essential to him as a man to have had a right will, and so to have avoided moral sin.

In the philosophy that we are considering, only the contemplative and active lives are reckoned human. The life of pleasure only, one of which the end is pleasure, is subhuman; every animal "knows what it likes," and seeks for it. This is not an exclusion of pleasure from life as if pleasure were wrong in itself, it is an exclusion of the pursuit of pleasure thought of as a "diversion," and apart from "life." It is in life itself, in "proper operation," that pleasure arises naturally, and this very pleasure is said to "perfect the operation" itself. It is the same way in the case of the pleasures of use or the understanding of use.

We need hardly say that from the traditional point of view there could hardly be found a stronger condemnation of the present social order than in the fact that the man at work is no longer doing what he likes best, but rather what he must, and in the general belief that a man can only be really happy when he "gets away" and is at play. For even if we mean by "happy" to enjoy the "higher things of life," it is a cruel error to pretend that this can be done at leisure if it has not been done at work. For "the man devoted to his own vocation finds perfection . . . That man whose prayer and praise of God are in the doing of his own work perfects himself."[2] It is this way of life that our civilization denies to the vast majority of men, and in this respect that it is notably inferior to even the most primitive of savage societies with which it can be contrasted.

MANUFACTURE, the practice of an art, is thus not only the production of utilities but in the highest possible sense the education of men. But we have forgotten what we are, what "man" in this philosophy denotes, a spiritual as well as a psychophysical being. We are therefore well contented with a functional art, good of its kind insofar as goodness does not interfere with profitable salability, and can hardly understand how things to be used can also have a meaning. It is true that what we have come to understand by "man," *viz.*, "the reasoning and mortal animal," can live by "bread alone," and that bread alone, make no mistake about it, is therefore a good; to function is the very least that can be expected of any work of art. "Bread alone" is the same thing as a "merely functional art." But when it is said that man does not live by bread alone but "by every word that proceedeth out of the mouth of God,"[3] it is the whole man that is meant. The "words of God" are precisely those ideas and principles that can be expressed whether verbally or visually by art; the words or visual forms in which they are expressed are not merely sensible but also significant. To separate as we do the functional from the significant art, applied from a so-called fine art, is to require of the vast majority of men to live by the merely functional art, a "bread alone" that is nothing but the "husks that the swine did eat."

Primitive man, despite the pressure of his struggle for existence, knew nothing of such merely functional arts. The whole man is naturally a metaphysician, and only later on a philosopher and psychologist, a systematist. His reasoning is by analogy, or in other words by means of an "adequate symbolism." As a person rather than an animal he knows immortal through mortal things. That

the "invisible things of God" (that is to say, the ideas or eternal reasons of things, by which we know what they ought to be like) are to be seen in "the things that are made"[4] applied for him not only to the things that God had made but to those that he made himself. He could not have thought of meaning as something that might or might not be added to useful objects at will. Primitive man made no real distinction of sacred from secular: his weapons, clothing, vehicles and house were all of them imitations of divine prototypes, and were to him even more what they meant than what they were in themselves; he made them this "more" by incantation and by rites. Thus he fought with thunderbolts, put on celestial garments, rode in a chariot of fire, saw in his roof the starry sky, and in himself more than "this man" So-and-so. All these things belonged to the "Lesser Mysteries" of the crafts, and to the knowledge of "Companions."

To have seen in his artifacts nothing but the things themselves,

and in the myth a mere anecdote, would have been a mortal sin, for this would have been the same as to see in oneself nothing but the "reasoning and mortal animal," to recognize only "this man," and never the "form of humanity." It is just insofar as we do now see only the things as they are in themselves, and only ourselves as we are in ourselves, that we have killed the metaphysical man and shut ourselves up in the dismal cave of functional and economic determinism.

IN ALL RESPECTS the traditional artist devotes himself to the good of the work to be done. The operation is a rite, the celebrant neither intentionally nor even consciously expressing himself. It is by no accident of time, but in accordance with a governing concept of the meaning of life, of which the goal is implied in St. Paul's *Vivo autem jam non ego*,[5] that works of traditional art, whether Christian, Oriental, or folk art, are hardly ever signed: the artist is anonymous, or if a name has survived, we know little or nothing of the man. This is true as much for literary as for plastic artifacts. In traditional arts it is never *Who said?* but only *What was said?* that concerns us: for "all that is true, by whomsoever it has been said, has its origin in the Spirit."[6]

So the first sane questions that can be asked about a work of art are, *What was it for?* and *What does it mean?* We have seen already that whatever, and however humble, the functional purpose of the work of art may have been, it had always a spiritual meaning, by no means an arbitrary meaning, but one that the function itself expresses adequately by analogy. Function and meaning cannot be forced apart; the meaning of the work of art is its intrinsic form as much as the soul is the form of the body.

The anonymity of the artist belongs to a type of culture dominated by the longing to be liberated from oneself. All the force of this philosophy is directed against the delusion "I am the doer." "I" am not in fact the doer, but the instrument; human individuality is not an end but only a means. The supreme achievement of individual consciousness is to lose or find (both words mean the same) itself in what is both its first beginning and its last end: "Whoever would save his *psyche*, let him lose it."[7] All that is required of the instrument is efficiency and obedience; it is not for the subject to aspire to the throne; the constitution of man is not a democracy, but the hierarchy of body, soul, and spirit. Is it for the Christian to consider any work "his own," when even Christ has said that "I do nothing of myself"?[8] or for the Hindu, when Krishna has said that "the Comprehensor cannot form the concept 'I am the doer'"?[9] or the Buddhist, for whom it has been said that "to wish that it may be made known that 'I was the author' is the thought of a man not yet adult"?[10] It hardly occurred to the individual artist to sign his works, unless for practical purposes of distinction; and we find the same conditions prevailing in the scarcely yet defunct community of the Shakers, who made perfection of workmanship a part of their religion, but made it a rule that works should not be signed. It is under such conditions that a really living art, unlike what Plato calls the arts of flattery, flourishes; and where the artist exploits his own personality and becomes an exhibitionist that art declines.

THE PLAIN MAN has no use for art unless he knows what it is about, or what it is for. And so far, this is perfectly right; if it is not about something, and not for anything, it *has* no use. And furthermore, unless it is about something *worthwhile*—more worthwhile, for example, than the artist's precious personality—and for something worthwhile to the patron and consumer as well as to the artist and maker, it has no *real* use, but is only a luxury product or mere ornament. On these grounds art may be dismissed by a religious man as mere vanity, by the practical man as an expensive superfluity, and by the class thinker as part and parcel of the whole bourgeoisie fantasy. There are thus two opposite points of view, of which one asserts that there can be no good use without art, the other that art is a superfluity. Observe, however, that these contrary statements are affirmed with respect to two very different things, which are not the same merely because both have been called "art." Let us now take for granted the historically normal and religiously orthodox view that, just as ethics is the "right way of doing things," so art is the "making well of whatever needs making," or simply "the right way of making things"; and still addressing ourselves to those for whom the arts of personality are superfluous, ask whether art is not after all a necessity.

A necessity is something that we cannot afford to do without, whatever its price. We cannot go into questions of price here, except to say that art need not be and should not be expensive, except to the extent that costly materials are employed. It is at this point that the crucial question arises of manufacture for profit versus manufacture for use. It is because the idea of manufacture for profit is bound up with the currently accepted industrial sociology that things in general are not well made and therefore also not beautiful. It is the manufacturer's interest to produce what we like, or can be induced to like, regardless of whether or not it will agree with us; like other modern artists, the manufacturer is expressing himself, and only serving our real needs to the extent that he *must* do so in order to be able to sell at all. It is only when the maker of things is a maker of things by vocation, and not merely holding down a job, that the price of things is approximate to their real value; and under these circumstances, when we pay for a work of art designed to serve a necessary purpose, we get our money's worth; and the purpose being a necessary one, we *must* be able to afford to pay for the art, or else are living below a normal human standard; as most men are now living, even the rich, if we consider quality rather than quantity. Needless to add that the workman is also victimized by a manufacture for profit; so that it has become a mockery to say to him that hours of work should be more enjoyable than hours of leisure; that when at work he should be doing what he likes, and only when at leisure doing what he ought—workmanship being conditioned by art, and conduct by ethics.

INDUSTRY WITHOUT art is brutality. Art is specifically human. None of those primitive peoples, past or present, whose culture we affect to despise and propose to amend, has dispensed with art; from the Stone Age onwards, everything made by man, under whatever conditions of hardship or poverty, has been made by art to serve a double purpose, at once utilitarian and ideological. It is we who, collectively speaking at least, command amply sufficient resources, and do not shrink from wasting these resources, who have first proposed to make a division of art, one sort to be barely utilitarian, the other luxurious, and altogether omitting what was once the highest function of art, to express and communicate ideas. It is long since sculpture was thought of as the poor man's "book." Our very word "aesthetics," from *aesthesis* (feeling), proclaims the dismissal of the intellectual values of art. A real art is one of symbolic and significant representation, a representation of things that cannot be seen except by the intellect. In Plato's words, "We cannot give the name of art to anything irrational."

A traditional must not be confused with an academic or merely fashionable art. A traditional art has fixed ends and ascertained means of operation, has been transmitted from teacher to pupil from an immemorial past, and retains its values even when it has quite gone out of fashion. All traditional art is a folk art in the sense that it is the art of a unanimous people. Where the thread of symbolic and initiatory teaching has been broken at higher social levels (and modern education, whether in India or elsewhere, has precisely and very often intentionally this destructive effect), it is just the "superstitions" of the people and what is apparently irrational in religious doctrine that has preserved what would otherwise have been lost. When the bourgeoisie culture of the universities has thus declined to levels of purely empirical and factual information, then it is precisely and only in the superstitions of the peasantry, wherever these have been strong enough to resist the subversive efforts of the educators, that there survives a genuinely human and often, indeed, a superhuman wisdom, however unconscious, and however fragmentary and naive may be the form in which it is expressed. What has really been preserved in folk and fairy tales and in popular peasant art is by no means a body of merely childish or entertaining fables or of crude decorative art, but a series of what are really esoteric doctrines and symbols of anything but popular invention. One may say that it is in this way, when an intellectual decadence has taken place in higher circles, that this doctrinal material is preserved from one epoch to another, affording a glimmer of light in what may be called the dark night of the intellect; the folk memory serving the purpose of a sort of ark in which the wisdom of a former age is carried over the period of the dissolution of cultures that takes place at the close of a cycle.

NOTES

1. *Per artem et ex voluntate* (Thomas Aquinas, *Sum. Theol.* I.45.6.)
2. Bhagavad-Gītā, *XVIII*, 45-6.
3. Matthew 4:4.
4. Romans 1:20.
5. Galatians 2:20. "I live; yet not I . . ."
6. Ambrose on 1 Cor. 12:3, cited by Thomas Aquinas, *Sum. Theol.* I-II.109.
7. cf. Luke 17:33.
8. John 8:28.
9. Bhagavad-Gītā, *III*-27.
10. Dhammapada, 74.

From Ananda K. Coomaraswamy, Christian and Oriental Philosophy of Art *(New York: Dover, 1956).*

EPICYCLE

The Story of Arachne/Greek

IN THE LAND of Lydia there lived a maiden, Arachne by name, who was a weaver. Born to humble parents—her father was a dyer of wool—Arachne was put to work on the loom as a young girl. From the start, she seemed to have a gift; she worked diligently and learned the craft well, so well that her skill soon surpassed that of the other village weavers. Daily she sat at the loom turning out tapestry and cloth, each piece more beautiful than the last, brilliant in color with fine, seamless texture that was remarkable in its perfection. She became the most skillful of mortals and her fame as a weaver spread far and wide.

People came from everywhere, not just to see Arachne's finished creations but to watch the intricate pictures take shape in the warp and weft as she worked. Even the nymphs who served the gods admired her deftness with shuttle and comb, and word of it drifted back to Olympus and to Athena.

Pallas Athena, goddess of war and wisdom, who sprang full-formed from the forehead of Zeus, had brought numerous gifts to mankind. It was she who planted the prized olive, which won her the city of Athens, and she who taught men how to tame horses. She was also the goddess of handicraft, originating pottery and leatherwork—she invented the bridle—and carpentry, used by Jason to build the great ship Argo. A shaper of metals, she fashioned the flute and the trumpet. But her greatest renown was as a textile maker. Athena taught women to spin, embroider, and weave. The tapestries from her loom were exquisite to the last detail, woven in colors vivid or subtle according to the subject. Her diverse skills were known and respected by all the Immortals; none surpassed her in these accomplishments, nor, indeed, would the goddess have allowed it.

As Arachne's fame increased so did the pride she took in her prowess. One day, when she had completed her most beautiful creation, a nymph complimented the work and said admiringly, "It is magnificent, Arachne, you must have been taught by Athena herself."

"Not at all," replied Arachne. "I taught myself." And looking closely at the piece, noting with satisfaction that not a thread was out of place, she continued, "I daresay that there is nothing more that I could learn from her."

The nymph was shocked to hear such words. "Take care, Arachne, no mortal can compete with a goddess!" she said. But Arachne replied, "I have seen her work, and my weaving is as fine and flawless as anything she has done. Perhaps we should have a contest, to see who is better." When word of Arachne's challenge came to Athena, the goddess was amazed at the girl's temerity. What could she be thinking of, not to recognize the source of her gift? Disguising herself as an old crone, the goddess went to Arachne to try and persuade her to withdraw her arrogant challenge.

Bent and gray, supporting herself with a stick, the goddess approached Arachne at her loom. She watched for a time until the girl looked up. "Greetings, my dear," said the old woman, "I have come to give you a bit of friendly advice. It is one thing to be supreme among mortals in your skill, but surely you know it does not pay to challenge a goddess. Athena has heard and is angry, but if you withdraw your challenge and apologize, she will forgive you and you will avoid much sorrow."

But proud Arachne remained defiant. "Go along, old woman," she said with disdain. "What do you know, and who are you to offer such warning to me? I know what I can do. Why does Athena not come herself and prove she is a better weaver than I? Perhaps she is afraid to do so." At this, the old woman threw off her cloak and assumed her true form as the goddess. The two faced one another, Pallas in all her majesty, and Arachne, flushed but unbowed. "I have come," said Athena. "Let us begin."

SUDDENLY THERE WERE yarns and threads of every hue piled about them, only the richest and rarest, of colors as subtle as the rainbow, as vibrant as the sunset. People crowded as close as they dared, to watch. The goddess and the girl set to work quickly. Their fingers flew as they drew the shuttles through the taut threads, weaving the most intricate tapestries each could devise. Athena wove the stories of the gods in all their splendor and magnificence: Poseidon with his trident rising from the ocean, Zeus on his throne on Olympus, and she herself in helmet and aegis planting the olive on the acropolis. At each corner, as a warning to Arachne for her audacity, she wove stories of other foolish mortals who had challenged Olympus and suffered for their insolence. Lastly, around the tapestry's border she embroidered olives, her own tree and the symbol of peace.

Arachne chose to depict the love affairs and peccadilloes of the gods, mocking the Olympians with her clever portrayals of their trysts and seductions,

weaving in also examples of how the wayward gods tricked and cheated mortals.

When they had finished, the tapestries were placed side by side. People were stunned to see how perfect and vividly rendered they were, but they gasped at Arachne's brazen scenes. Athena was enraged by the girl's defiance. She examined Arachne's work minutely but could find no fault or flaw in it. This only increased her fury. She took Arachne's tapestry and rent it in two. Then she took her wooden shuttle and beat the girl mercilessly. Arachne crept away, defeated, and procuring a noose, she fastened it around her neck, and hanged herself.

But the goddess came to her and lifted her up, saying, "No, Arachne, you shall not die. You shall continue to hang by a thread for the rest of your life—and your descendants will do likewise—as a reminder of your impious deed." Athena then brought forth a vial containing the juice of an herb which she sprinkled on the girl. Immediately the maiden began to shrink; her hair turned gray and covered her entire body. Her face, except for the eyes, disappeared, and her limbs wizened to become the spindly legs of a spider. The rope from which she dangled became the silken thread which to this day the spider draws out of her belly to spin her web.

—Retold by Barbara Ensrud

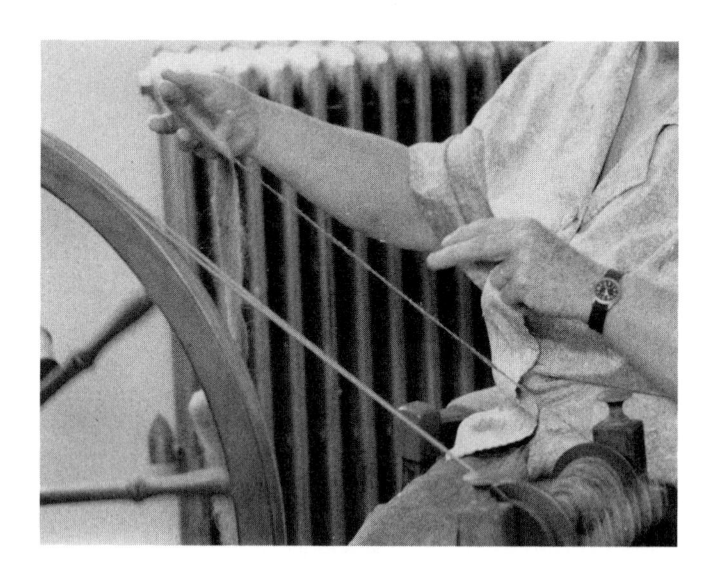

Spinning: Leaving Well Alone

AN INTERVIEW WITH BARBARA WHEELER

Photographs by Lee B. Ewing

Barbara Wheeler is a handspinner who lives on a small farm in Chester, New Jersey, where she breeds sheep for their wool. Her education as a zoologist, her experience with mill processing and wool grading, and her upbringing in England have contributed to her perspective as a craftsman. She has given workshops over the past fifteen years on a variety of subjects connected with handspinning both to small guilds and at national conferences. Based on her belief that fine materials themselves inform the craftsman, she runs a small business providing fibers to handspinners across the country. We recently visited her at her farm, where she demonstrated the craft of spinning as she spoke to us.

—The Editors

PARABOLA: For this issue of PARABOLA, we are interested in the transformation of the material of craft and how the craftsman relates to both that process and to another transformation, in himself. As a spinner and weaver, how do you look at this? It seems that there is a very long process in the change of wool, from its production on the animal, through carding, spinning, dyeing, to the woven piece of fabric.

BARBARA WHEELER: It goes even beyond that, you know. Sheep would not have wool as we know it today but for man's intervention, in lengthening it and making it more suitable for spinning. Primitive sheep had practically no wool, just a heavy pelt, and there are still some woolless breeds. One can say that man's interaction with sheep produced the wool, in a certain sense. The first spinners

used the molted fibers from sheep, the way we did in England during the war, when we used fibers found on the hedgerows to make socks for the soldiers.

P: Could you describe your acquaintance with the whole process? You raise sheep and produce different kinds of fleeces. What is your work, as a craftsperson, in raising sheep?

BW: I have a very small flock, and I am trying to produce a certain type of wool which is extremely difficult to find. If they can get two colors of wool of matching quality, handspinners can use it very creatively; it is very appealing. Unfortunately, the quality of fiber from individual animals can be quite different, especially that of colored animals, even when they are mother and daughter.

P: What exactly is the quality you are trying to get in your sheep? What do you mean by "quality"?

BW: In this case, I am trying to get colored wools of high luster, with extremely fine diameter of fiber, soft handle, and good length. It is easy enough to get luster and coarse long fibers. Fine high-luster wool is characteristic of breeds such as Wensleydale and Teeswater which are used in England for crossing to improve the length and quality on rough hill breeds. Rams of these breeds are sold only after they have proved that they can produce good crossbred lambs. In this country the emphasis is on purebred animals, whereas in England intentionally hybrid ewes are the basis of the commercial lamb-producing flocks.

P: Is breeding then the only way you can affect the production of this special wool, or is there anything in the feeding, or environment?

BW: Basically, if I had more land, I would have chosen a breed to suit the land first, then improved the wool on that breed because it suits the land. Sheep exist all over the world, and are produced in many different ways. There are many different forms of husbandry. For example, traditional Middle Eastern flocks are taken from place to place in a yearly cycle; in Switzerland the flocks go up to pasture in the summer and come down in winter; the island populations are out all year round; and in Iceland the sheep are confined in winter and let out in the summer. Each type of husbandry and geographic area has characteristic breeds with their own style of wool. After all, the wool must first cover the sheep and protect it from the elements. From these differences wools have been developed in amazingly wide variety from the finest Merino to the coarsest carpet wools, each with its own special uses.

P: So husbandry is very important—and midwifery too. It seems that to be a midwife is a good metaphor for a craftsperson.

BW: It is true, in the sense that one leaves well alone. One has to watch, but not interfere. I had a case recently which took me far more time than I like to give. A young ewe was in trouble—by what means I knew that she was in trouble, I don't know, just something wasn't quite right. She gave birth to a lamb which unfortunately died. It appeared normal, but from the first, something was wrong. Maybe it was premature. I had to not interfere, because in fact, to be practical, I don't need that sheep, I don't need that lamb.

P: It is the principle of letting nature take care of its own.

BW: Exactly. So, when I am building up a flock, I can't afford to keep an animal that is not going to pay its way, no matter how beautiful the fleece. A ewe either produces a lamb and wool is profit, or she produces wool and the lamb is profit—one or the other. A ram represents half the herd, so the choice of a ram is very important. His influence is expressed in every lamb in its quality of wool, its health and vigor as well as its future productivity.

P: Could you describe the process of spinning the wool?

BW: Early spinning was probably done by rolling the fibers on the thigh, but these people found that as soon as they let go, the fibers would unspin. Then somebody discovered that you actually had to wind those fibers into a ball if you were going to continue making a long strand. So they learned how to either wind those fibers onto something, a spindle, or two people would spin between them, with one winding the thread up in a ball. Some primitive people found a way to spin two strands across the thigh, and then bring them back, making a double ply. I can show that here, if I allow a spun single thread to wind back onto itself, it is a natural ply. When I break it off from the rest of the strand, the spin will not disappear. When I break off a single spun piece, it immediately comes undone. One sees there is a kind of balancing of forces in the yarn. Traditionally, many yarns are made of plied wool, particularly for knitting, because a knitted single ply pills more, for some reason. Also, when you knit a single ply wool there will be a skew in your fabric. The Peruvians used to use single plies, some spun one direction, some spun the other direction, in order to avoid this. It was partially for design purposes, but it was more fundamentally for making the fabric more stable. The double ply allows the forces in both strands to be balanced,

One sees there is a kind of balancing of forces in the yarn.

and a long strand can be made without having to be wound up on anything. Wool is also made in skeins, which means the yarn is wrapped around and around, and then the two ends are tied together, which prevents the twist coming off.

P: What actually happens to the wool when it is spun?

BW: The basic principle of spinning is making short discrete fibers into something that has a usefulness, a tensile strength in a continuous strand. The process by which that is done is by twisting the fibers. What happens when those fibers are twisted? If you twist an unprepared lock of wool, it just becomes a big fat twist, and when you let go, it comes undone. So it is something more than just twisting. You've got many fibers, and they all have cut ends in one place. In order to extend the length, you have to spread the ends out, so there is a drawing out process which is involved. Then you can twist the fibers into a continuous strand. But then you face the problem—what to do when you have to let go? The strand still has to be put somewhere, to be stabilized. So implements, tools were invented to make it possible for those fibers to be spun in a continuous length.

P: What is the process that prepares the wool before it is spun?

BW: In a prepared rollag of wool, all the fibers have been separated and mixed up lengthwise, either by hand or machine. This process is called carding, which consists of separating and disarraying the fibers so that all the cut ends don't come in the same place, and then rearranging and making them more or less lengthwise in the strand. A machine-prepared rollag has also been drawn, which helps to make those fibers go more lengthwise.

P: Could you show us how you spin?

BW: [*She begins to spin and continues speaking.*] In teaching spinning, I learned a great deal, because when you try to show anything, it never works. In order to show some of the processes of spinning, for instance, how the lumps will even out—if you watch carefully, you will see the strand is actually becoming more even—you can't show it unless you're spinning. You have to be actually working and attending in your hands to what you are doing, and at the same time, speaking. When I first started to spin and teach, I realized that I was lying, because I was not doing what I said I was doing. One is not actually as knowledgeable about what one is doing as one thinks one is. The question has to remain: What is actually going on? I kept on finding myself saying "But, but, but . . . you see . . ." because much more was going on than I was able to describe.

So, to come back to the essence of what is happening right now: If you notice how my hands are when I'm spinning, there is a triangle here [*between her hand holding the rollag and the emerging spun strand*]. This is where spinning is actually taking place, and where these forces which I'm interested in are working. Here the spin is in the thread and prevents it from pulling out. Nearer to my hand, it will pull out. I am attending to this place, not by sight, but by feel. If you watch me when I'm spinning, you'll see I'm doing all sorts of things just in this area. My hand has many possible movements, which are always working, responding to the feel of the draw of the wool. Now I'm controlling how the fibers go into that triangle with my thumb. I can also move my hand around in many ways. The triangle has to feel just right and allow just the right amount of fibers into the yarn. The movements of my hand are continually working. The forces are involved in that place, right here; there is a force which just does not exist if you are not pulling back against the pull in, which is being exerted by the wheel.

P: It is a wonderful example of the necessity of resistance, isn't it?

BW: There is a book of photographs of the whirling dervishes. The introduction describes the image of a spinner taking fibers from a source above him and making a thread by twisting a spindle—symbolically the dervish is spinning a thread to heaven. It seems to me that there are many interesting things in that, like what you said about the necessity of resistance. But in order to create the thread at all, something has to be, as it were, aligned upward. Something has also to really *happen*. It is not as simple as a "doing"—he is not really *making* a thread to heaven, it is being made, just as this thread is an expression of forces which I have to allow to happen.

The force that brings the thread together is something that fascinates me, because one doesn't really under-

stand it. Even in commerce, they don't understand it. What is the action of the twist? You see it here, but can you tell me what it is? I can't. But without a doubt, if you twist this fiber, something is pulled into the center, and the fiber coheres. The force is most easily shown when I join, you can see how the fibers are brought in. People don't trust that, they try to make it happen, by winding it around, and it doesn't work. The force is there, but it's only there when you are pulling back, resisting. Then two forces meet, as it were, and there is this twist, which brings in more fiber, in a spiral.

P: But the two forces have to meet through your hand. If your hand wasn't there, they would not meet.

BW: Yes, exactly.

P: I can't see your hand moving at all! Are you going at a slower tempo, to show me? And when you teach do you go at a slower tempo?

The force that brings the thread together is something that fascinates me.

BW: You have to.

P: But one can see that the tempo also changes according to the wool. Does the place where the spinning is happening also change?

BW: Yes. It is always moving, and one is attending continually to a moving place on the thread. My hand is doing all the work, but is concerned with the feel of the tensile strength of the thread. When I begin to spin, or when I have to start with a new rollag, I have to join the new piece to the end of the previous one. In joining, again my hands are concerned with the tension of the old and the new. Until they become the same, the join will not be strong. I always say that you should be absolutely happy to break and rejoin the yarn. Until you are, your joins aren't secure and strong. Of course, if you were using handcarded wool, you would have to join your yarn again and again, because the handcards were designed to make small rollags. I've even heard someone complain that they couldn't join so they tied each strand.

There are many styles of spinning of more or less validity. Each may be suitable in one situation for a particular type of fiber. Traditional methods have stood the test of time and are more widely applicable. In the same way there are many ways of preparing fibers for spinning, each designed towards a particular end, handcarding, handcombing, teasing, and so on. Each enhances a particular quality in the yarn, bringing to the fore the warmth, softness, strength, or luster, for instance.

P: When and where did you learn to spin?

BW: I would say that I learned more from handling different wools than I ever learned from a teacher. I was taught how to spin, the basics of it, but really I did not learn what I know now except through exchange with other spinners and the material. I would really say I learned to spin from the material.

P: Could you give some examples of that?

BW: The material has to be right for the use and rightly prepared, from the sheep's back, as it were. There is almost always a compromise, because one rarely gets the opportunity to produce something from basic material. This wool that I have in my hand is a compromise. It is Shetland wool which used to be plucked from the sheep because the sheep molts. If you look at the wool, you will find little short pieces, which is the difference between the point where they sheared the sheep and the natural molt line. It's a weak place. This wool has its use, because for "handcraft" purposes, people like the "handspun" look—the unevenness, the slight noils in the yarn, are what people like. They don't like the absolutely dead look of commercial yarns, and not many people are subtle enough to appreciate the fine quality of strong, even fibers prepared and spun to an even strand. We are not free, as handspinners, of the constraints of available material and of taste. It is not easy to sell plain, beautifully even, fine yarn. Many handspinners aspire to make that kind of yarn, but there is little market for it.

P: You yourself also weave. Nowadays, it is probably a luxury to weave things for yourself. But as it started out, people spun and wove, not to sell things, but to make and use them. How do the different ways of spinning that you are speaking of affect the finished product that *you* make?

BW: I will spin according to the need I have for a particular piece. If I want warm wool, I will spin something like this Shetland, and will accept some of the unevenness, for the sake of the insulating qualities that come from the air in the wool. If I want to have something for upholstery, I would choose a different wool and be much more concerned with the smoothness and evenness and strength of the yarn. This yarn, though it is very strong, is not as strong as it could be if I put more twist on it. [*She demonstrates by putting more spin on the yarn she has already spun.*] You will see what happens to the yarn—it becomes more compact—and then it is also much stronger. If I go even further, the forces on the fiber are so strong that it becomes distorted, it will actually become brittle. It crinkles up and becomes unusable.

P: Even in face of these incomprehensible things like twist, or resistance, or spirals, it seems that there is a link in the craftsman's hand. The body is able to comprehend these forces. What then is the role of the mind?

BW: It is there to try to understand. When people learn how to spin, they are taught a certain method, as I was taught. I have been showing spinning for some time, and sometimes people will come up to me and say, "That is not how it is done. That is not how you spin." They were taught a different method or style. Yet it is patently obvious that *I am spinning*. Without trying to understand what is happening, it can be mindless imitation and won't go far.

P: Today, I have been watching you spin, but I have not learned how to spin.

BW: You will not learn how by explanation—you can't. The Navajos, for instance, show, but they never teach. You would need to try.

P: Is weaving at all the same sort of tensile experience that you have spoken of? Could you describe it?

BW: It can be understood in particular when you set up a loom. You have all these threads, and you have to get the tension absolutely even. If you try to make each thread the same tension, you are not able to do it, thread by thread. But if you pass your fingers right across, as a friend of mine has put it, "playing the harp," you can feel if one thread is out of kilter. You can feel if it is tighter. If it is, you let it off, try again, and let it off, until it is more or less the same. Then you feel a whole group of threads, and you let them find their own tension. You run your hand up and down the group again and again, and then you refasten them, and feel again. It is a process of the threads gradually coming to an even tension. Skillful weavers do that without any problem. As they wind their threads onto a warping board or a warping mill, they are aware of the tension in the threads. Maybe they don't know with their minds, in a way that we expect to know, but they're paying attention to that tension on the threads at all times, just as I am when I spin.

P: I think that a common conception of spinning or weaving is that it must be a very "relaxing" or peaceful thing to do. Would you describe it that way?

BW: Is paying attention quietly to something that you are doing peaceful?

P: It is very different from what people usually call relaxing. The sense of well-being that comes to you comes from paying attention, from allowing the attention to be centered in a different place from where it usually is.

BW: In other activities, one's focus is very often visual, one is thinking only in terms of what one can see, yet there are a number of blind spinners who may even have an advantage because they are directly involved with the sense of touch.

Spinning and weaving have very little component of sound, but a strong component of rhythm. The rhythm of both spinning and weaving allows one to attend in a different

There is a delight in producing something that is absolutely appropriate to its use.

---

way. By becoming aware of the beginning and end of a phrase, which is quite different from one's usual concept of "moment to moment," you can see the thing as a whole. The attention is centered, and also broadened.

P: In the usual way of "attending," where everything is concentrated in mental activity, the body becomes unevenly involved in the movement. Watching you spin, one can see that it is the whole body that is involved, not just the hands. There is movement also in your feet, and your shoulders, and your head—everything participates in the movement. Therefore those parts of the body, by being involved, are probably much more relaxed than they usually are when one is just thinking about something.

BW: There is no question about it.

P: How do you work with these two colors of wool, in the spinning and weaving processes?

BW: As a spinner, I try to be colorblind, at times, so as not to try to make the different colors come as I wish them to, but to allow them to occur on their own.

P: That is very different from weaving, where you have to plan the color, isn't it?

BW: That is entirely different, but there is a place for both. You may take a random, colorblind, selection of threads or a strict order of colors. The threads woven across may also reflect a repeated order and give a precise woven pattern or be random as well, giving a shadowy effect. An unevenly spun yarn blending two or more colors will soften a woven design so that it blurs or drifts in and out sometimes in a very beautiful way. I did a whole series of studies where I used two colors and put them into a knitted Fair Isle design, one of which was the basic color, and another a blended color against it. The effect was sometimes heart-rendingly beautiful, and sometimes just dull, depending on the choice and proportion of the colors in the blend.

P: How do you feel about what you make, whether it is the thread or a woven piece? How important is that to the craftsman, what is actually made, or is it the process itself that interests you more?

BW: There is a delight in producing something that is absolutely appropriate to its use, whether it's a yarn or a piece. When I say appropriate, I mean the quality—the feel, the handle of the piece of fabric—the design, and the long-term wearing quality. It should be absolutely appropriate for what it is intended. I feel that there is a kind of balance between experiment and exploration, and something more rigid which can only come from foreseeing as far as I am capable. There exists far more in terms of appropriateness than I can really encompass. I think it was Hamada who said "I collect pieces that either overwhelm me technically—I just can't see how they are done—or something that touches me gently in the heart." ●

EPICYCLE

The Patience of Penelope/Greek

Penelope watched and waited for Odysseus to come back from the long war for Troy. Years passed, Telemachus her son grew from childhood to young manhood, and then one day false rumors spread throughout the lands that Odysseus was dead. Because Penelope was still young, beautiful, and wealthy besides, suitors flocked to Ithaca to try to win her favors. But she did not respond to their flattery or their foolish antics; her grief for Odysseus was too great. Instead, she withdrew to her rooms, where hour after hour the only sounds to be heard were the whirring and click of her spinning wheel as she filled spindle after spindle with ever softer and finer strands of wool.

The suitors grew restless. The more she ignored them, the more they made themselves at home, devouring her food and emptying her wine cellars. The turning of Penelope's troubled thoughts began to accompany the turning of the spinning wheel as she realized her helplessness. With no husband to defend her and Telemachus still too young to send the suitors on their way, what was she to do? Then one day, as she passed by the loom which was in the great hall, she had an idea. She came to the suitors and told them that she would choose one from among them, but only after she finished weaving all the wool that she had spun. Laertes, the father of Odysseus, was old and frail, and she wished to weave his funeral shroud before she married again. The suitors sympathized with her wishes, and Penelope sat down at her loom.

Each day the first to wake would find her already at work weaving intricate patterns with subtle blendings of detail and color. The work proceeded slowly, and the suitors waited day after day, season after season. What they did not know was that every night, when the last merrymaker fell silent and began to snore, Penelope would creep softly to the loom and unravel most of the work she had done the previous day. Two years passed into three, and three into four, and still the weaving was not complete.

In this way Penelope practiced her craft to deceive the suitors until her labors were rewarded by the return of Odysseus. It was not a simple homecoming: many more stories are told about how the hero disguised himself and entered his stronghold by stealth and wile; how he hid himself among the suitors and discovered the full extent of their treachery; how he learned of Penelope's suffering and faithfulness during his long absence; and finally how he revealed himself, fought a mighty battle, and turned the suitors out of the house. Amid the joyful noise of feasting and triumphal celebrations, Penelope abandoned her loom for her husband's arms.

—Retold by Ellen Draper

Some Notes on Arab Calligraphy

Jean Sulzberger

PLATO WROTE, "Writing is the geometry of the spirit, and it manifests itself by means of the organs of the body."

And the Arab calligraphers say, "The essence of writing is in the spirit, even though it is manifested by means of the limbs."

The harmony one feels in Arab calligraphy comes from specific rules that are followed, so that knowledge and presence as well as a disciplined hand are required. Calligraphy is a spiritual exercise. The calligraphers teach that when a man is inwardly free, his writing is good. Disciples of master calligraphers have to undergo fasts and a long training to purify themselves before they can write. "Purity of writing is purity of soul," it is said.

Ali, the fourth Caliph, was a calligrapher, and other followers of Muhammad were known as *Sahib al-sayf wa al-qalam* (masters of the sword and the pen). "God first created the *qalam* [the pen]," Muhammad said.

Everything connected with the calligraphers' art has significance, beginning with the *qalam*. Several kinds of trimmed reed pens play as important a role in calligraphy as voices do in song. After a sharp knife makes a point in the *qalam*, the point is then split lengthwise into two parts "so that when it is put to paper it should vibrate and a ringing be heard." The part nearer the thumb, when the pen is held for writing, is called *unsī*, or human, and the other side is called *wahshī*, or wild.

The letters—there are twenty-eight letters in the Arabic alphabet—are said to be various aspects of human beings and animals. Each letter is spoken of as having a head, an eye, a nose, an arm, a leg, a trunk, or a tail. The letters are spoken of as being erect, straight, bent, standing, seated, good-looking, ugly, fat, tall, or short. For example, in the cursive scripts, the first letter, *alif*, is compared to a man standing up and looking down at his feet as if standing in prayer.

Disciples learn how to make the *qalam*, how to make it a good tool, how to make ink without fuss, the kind of paper to use, the colors to use to write in gold, how to make paste, how to polish the paper so that there are no creases in it, how to trim the *qalam* and clip its nib. They have to study the letters, to look at the "strengths and weaknesses" of the letters, to watch their "ascents and descents," and they have to prepare themselves before copying so that they can give it full attention. They are told to refrain from mistakes—"through mistakes no one will become someone."

O you who have not yet written one letter,
How can a master give you instruction?
For instruction in good writing
Cannot be given in your absence.
If the elements are hidden from you, and you yourself are absent,
Your objection has no sense.
Know that the theory of writing is shrouded,
And no one knows it until he has made an effort.
Until your teacher has told you by word of mouth,
You will not write with ease.
The means to impart some knowledge
Is both by writing and by word of mouth,
But know that the important thing is oral instruction
By which difficulties become easy.

—*From an eleventh-century Persian manuscript*

ARAB SOURCES say that the first man who wrote in Arabic and used the pen was Adam; after him Seth. Others say Abraham or Enoch invented writing. After the

The vertical lines correspond to a permanent inner structure.

Koranic revelation, Arabic script became the carrier of the revelation to the Muslim world. "The noblest of the visual arts in the world of Islam is calligraphy, and it is the writing of the Koran that is sacred art *par excellence*," Titus Burckhardt wrote. "It plays a part more or less analogous to that of the icon in Christian art, for it represents the visible body of the Divine Word."[1]

God says through His prophets, "Be!" (*kun*), and this command and all that issues from it was first written in the Koran in *jazm*, the earliest Arabic script, and the progenitor of the famous Kufic script. Kufic was followed in the tenth century by six major styles: *thuluth*, *naskh*, *muhaqqaq*, *rayhānī*, *tawqī'*, and *riqā'*. The styles are named after certain masters and schools. Kufic was named after the Iraqi city of Kufa where there was a school during the caliphate of Ali. In Kufic writing, one-sixth is circular and the rest is straight. Its horizontal and vertical lines look like squares and rectangles and are usually drawn with such geometric precision that the length and width and the distances separating them are equal. The Dome of the Rock in Jerusalem and the Alhambra Palace in Granada have Kufic inscriptions. *Thuluth* is the style often used for writing titles of chapters (*sūrahs*) in the Koran. *Naskhī*, a simpler, more rounded form than *thuluth*, is generally used in the body of Koranic texts. It is said that *thuluth* has the face of a grown-up and *naskhī* the face of an innocent boy.

Scripts that go into the writing of the Koran are also present in Islamic architecture, in tilework and woodwork, in pottery, inlaid bronzes, miniature paintings, and in the "zoomorphic" calligraphy that takes the shape of lions, camels, birds, or men.

The patterns of calligraphy, the distended, arched, or rounded letters endlessly reproducing themselves in a harmonious order that is somehow felt, are symbolic of the order of nature which in always changing is always repeating itself. The meandering horizontal lines are said to represent the continuity of life, and the vertical lines correspond to a permanent inner structure. "The richness of the Arabic script comes from the fact that it has fully developed its two 'dimensions': the vertical, which confers on the letters their hieratic dignity, and the horizontal, which links them together in a continuous flow," writes Burckhardt. "As in the symbolism of weaving, the vertical lines, analogous to the 'warp' of the fabric, correspond to the permanent essence of things—it is by the vertical that the unalterable character of each letter is affirmed—whereas the horizontal, analogous to the 'weft,' expresses becoming or the matter that links one thing to another."[2] •

NOTES

1. Titus Burckhardt, *Sacred Art in East and West* (London: Perennial Books, 1967), p. 116.
2. *Ibid.*

The Craft of a Contrary Man

Victor Hammer

Of his friend and publisher, Victor Hammer (1882-1967), Thomas Merton once wrote, "The art of Victor Hammer has in it not only the luminosity of classical technique, but the eloquence of classical myth."[1] *Hammer privately printed a number of Merton's shorter works for his Stamperia del Santuccio Press in Lexington, Kentucky (close by the Abbey of Gethsemani, where Merton spent his monastic years). But printing was only one of many skills that the Vienna-born painter and engraver excelled in, including making furniture and clavichords, bookbinding, calligraphy, and typography.*

Hammer was especially interested in the design and carving of type for hand-press printing, virtually a lost craft in the modern world. In The Forms of Our Letters *(posthumously published by Anvil Press, the successor of his Stamperia del Santuccio), he wrote: "Those visible marks, known as the Roman letter, are used for the purpose of recording speech. Each one of the twenty-six letters of the alphabet stands for a sound. The connection between sounds and visual symbols has to be known—and sounds when uttered in an established order are spoken language. In written language, therefore, letters have to follow one another in the same sequence as do sounds in speech. While speech sounds, once uttered, leave no trace, written letters remain visible."*[2]

In the following published dialogue with former student (and later patron) Edgar Kaufmann, Jr., Hammer begins by describing how he cuts the punches for the type he designs, then goes on to speak of his "contrary" dedication to the making of things in general in a traditional, more genuine, way. —*Paul Evans Holbrook*

CRAFTSMAN: Shanks of soft, cast steel, about two or three inches long, are ground in a facing block to procure a blank on one end. Then I shape the blank end of this steel shank into a negative letter form, using tools of hardened steel, such as burins and files. After it is finished I harden the soft shank, which then becomes a punch. A punch when driven into a flat piece of copper creates a mold, the matrix, from which the individual letters are cast. You may not be familiar with these technical terms; they are old terms used among craftsmen, and refer to the generative processes of life.

PATRON: Well—how many of these punches must you cut for a complete font of one size?

CRAFTSMAN: Fifty-two letters—not counting the accented letters—and about fifty signs make up every font. I am now cutting a new size of my "Uncial," and have just finished the lower case-letters which I always cut first, because this type is basically a minuscule and needs no capitals. For the last two versions of my type I have cut capitals to go with the minuscules, but the first font which was used for the Samson Agonistes contained only twenty-eight characters. This minuscule stems from a majuscule known as Uncial; it was not conceived as the lower-case letter of a customary font. The best way to attain a matured form of my type seemed to be to print books in it—small editions in several languages. As need arose I could modify certain letters in accord with the language of the text. The Samson Agonistes is one of those trials; it has no capitals. Capitals are a later addition to my Uncial, and though helpful they are not necessary.

PATRON: No, not necessary, but as all capitals ascend above the middle line, and as ascenders—and descenders as well—help us to read quickly, it was a good thing to introduce them. In ancient times scribes wrote in one continuous flow, stringing one character on to another line after line, like speech. But we have left script, and gone to print; our reading habits have changed, and "the ordinary man of our own times probably sees more printed and written matter in a week than the medieval scholar saw in a

year." You of course do not go along with the times, rather you oppose the trends and want to slow down reading. I gathered this from your paper: "A Dialogue on the Uncial."

CRAFTSMAN: Surely—I do not go with the times, nor do I go against them, for this would mean that I consider ephemera worth refuting. I am a craftsman, and as a craftsman I am expected to accept responsibility for the work I do with my hands. You wondered about the "mystical" quality of handiwork: it is that trace of life which lingers on in things made entirely by the human hand.

A letter written with a broad pen or a reed is a complete form; its inner and its outer contour, left and right, appear all at once as a form determined by the tool. In cutting a punch—say, of an O—I look at the in-

abcdefghijklmnopqr
stuvwxyz
ABCDEFGHIJKLMNOP
QRSTUVWXYZ
1234567890

ner form of the left curve while working at the outer form of the right curve, and vice versa. The secret of the craftsman's procedure is always to see details and distinctions in connection with the whole form he works upon. He doesn't know beforehand exactly what his work will look like—he will only know when it is finished. If a punch-cutter is alive to calligraphy, and to the task of reconciling changing forms of language with the unalterable forms of the Roman capital letter, by blending new letter combinations into a legible stream (the line), he will be able to cut his punches in as straightforward a manner as he would write a love letter or invoke the name of a god in an inscription. And then—his work will be alive.

The pantograph machine does away with the hand-cut punch. It engraves punches, and matrices as well. But since there is no craftsman, the machine calls for a "designer" and an "operator." Well, now you have a machine which cannot see and a designer who cannot carve: so he prepares an enlarged drawing of a letter—the design.

This drawing serves for making a template to be put into the machine, and when the power is turned on, someone (*i.e.*, the operator) moves a tracer point around its outlines, perhaps around the inner form first, then around the outer form, and a punch or a matrix is automatically engraved at the other end.

PATRON: Fine—and what's wrong with that? If you have a good design the type will be good too. I know you will say that the machine product cannot be alive. You haven't yet proved that a beautiful form turned out by the machine will in time lose its beauty because no human hand has endowed it with life. At least I am unable to see it that way. Besides, how can you hope, alone and isolated as you are, to turn the meaning of "design" back to its earlier, pre-industrial connotation?

CRAFTSMAN: Not while the international design conferences are in session. I don't expect to be heard during my lifetime, nor for a long time to come. Perhaps it would be better now to drop that topic.

PATRON: For the moment, yes. But we must come back to it. One's work and one's articles of faith belong to one another, though it is the work that carries the conviction. There is no doubt that you are fit for doing things with your hands, and that you like to finish them yourself. This may account for your aversion to the division of labor which the machine process necessitates. There is probably more than mere reasoning behind your insistence on the right methods of work as you call them—there was always an urge which drove you to the work bench.

CRAFTSMAN: Maybe. But it is difficult to trace such impulses back to their origin. Are they determined by one's earliest experiences, or have one's inclinations determined the experiences? Why do I remember things my father did, while he has forgotten them completely? When three or four, I was alone with him one day. Mother was out on an errand and had taken my older brother with her, but father continued to putter around the apartment we occupied. On his worktable he had a heavy iron block which he used as an anvil. It was a few inches wide and high, and on its top a die was sunk: an indented crown of five thorns with a bead on each of them. While he proceeded with his business of preparing some plaster of Paris, I was leaning against the trellis of the window, watching with interest the few horse-drawn carriages and wagons which every now and then were passing by. So I was not aware that he had poured some of the plaster into the hollows of the die, and when he called me back into the room and lifted a neatly cast crown of white plaster out of the die, I was surprised and enchanted. I must have said something to that effect. Whether it was about the precise, clearcut form or about the mysterious process of casting, I can't say for I do not remember. He too was surprised, and laughed at my response. He picked me up and hugged me in his arms. Now, I too have a workbench as you see, and I sink die after die: the punches for my Uncial type. It was a long, a lonely road which led from that first die in my conscious life to the books printed in the Uncial.

I did not create that type for aesthetic reasons (they don't exist for me), but language moved me to action. I was alive to calligraphy, and to the task of reconciling changing forms of language with the unchangeable forms of the Roman capital letter. I was in no hurry to produce the type. Therefore the pantograph machine and its moving arms could not hold me spellbound, nor did the fact that it can reduce a six-inch design to a four-point punch or matrix impress me unduly. There is mass production, but there can be no mass creation. The craftsman proceeds by methods different from the machine. A pot produced by the machine will hold as much water, and hold it as well as the craftsman's pot which, however, has the advantage that there is no designer between it and its maker. But the designer, who is neither fish nor fowl, a hybrid creature, will, one happy day, meet with his appropriate reward.

PATRON: But machines are perfect in themselves, admirable pieces of workmanship, conceived by the designer, and partly produced by machines. I won't insist that machines are alive, but they are useful and often good to look at, something one cannot say of too many people.

CRAFTSMAN: That's why one cannot blame the machine, only the people who use it. There is nothing wrong with the six-inch template, so long as one does not use it for making type. We are not yet ripe for conscious, farsighted restraint, at least not in matters we suppose to be harmless: we would consider it retrogression, not restraint.

PATRON: You know that I do not accept your theory of handicraft—not

because it is utterly inconceivable to go back to it, but because I cannot see a difference in quality between regularly shaped machine-made things, and irregularly shaped things done by hand. That we are not of the same generation may account for the difference in our viewpoints. Were it not for the profit motive on which industry hinges and expands (even when that motive is disguised), industry and handicrafts would not be incompatible. Only it would need a population of sages and saints to lure the handicrafts back into our lives; reformers couldn't do it. I am glad you like to be left alone, and that you leave others in peace—unregenerated. I know that you are largely self-taught . . .

CRAFTSMAN: *(interrupting)* . . . a good way to be taught; all other methods of teaching stem from it.

PATRON: You are a craftsman, and good at doing things with your hands—but your efforts to revive the handicrafts in our mechanical age seem to me completely mistaken. I just can't see it.

CRAFTSMAN: I agree, for I can't see it either. Those who are sensitive enough to resent the deadliness of machine-made things will continue to suffer, but may somehow manage to survive until they have created a shell of their own into which to retire, as I have done.

Through coercion one can be deprived of a lot of things, freedom and what not, but one cannot force upon people anything that is genuine or good—they have either to discover it themselves and pursue it deliberately or circumstances will teach them.

PATRON: Views such as yours originate in unusual personal experiences. Quite often you seem uncompromising and opinionated, but I think you are more tolerant than it appears, for I realize that you have never stubbornly and persistently pressed your arguments. If I were asked to write a summary of your views, I would head it—The Life and Opinions of a Contrary Man.

CRAFTSMAN: Well—that may be a good title for a book, and as an idea is quite attractive. However, does it do justice to what I said?—Do you remember Mnemosyne, the Greek goddess, and her daughters, the Muses?

The Muses taught man "to celebrate things that shall be and things that were aforetime"—they give aid to man's creative activity. Memory (Mnemosyne), their mother, wants to save what has been sung in praise of the gods, so that it may be handed down to posterity. In plainer words, and in guise of a warning: do not build and work only for the gratification of immediate needs, but build with the thought of a future life of the spirit on this earth. The thought of a life that continues after we as individuals are gone will purge our minds of selfish desires. If we don't want to be forgotten but want to live on, even anonymously, in the work we leave behind us, then let us work at the tokens of remembrance which Memory, the goddess, so badly needs. As a patron, or as an artist and a craftsman, you may be able to contribute to the spiritual life of mankind—for which we have a good though nowadays deflated word: human culture.

You labeled me the Contrary Man, but you did not say contrary to what. Truly, I am contrary to mediocrity, though I know we could not live on this planet without it; I am contrary to sloth, and contrary to waste, which will go on in spite of me, and I am contrary to blasphemy against the Spirit. I have proved to myself that I can change the world, but only within the reach of my hands. The work I leave behind me may not be great, yet it will prove to be genuine—genuine, though not "progressive." It may however show that I had to work alone most of the time. I am no reformer—and I know that I shall never see the day when the arts will again be a mode of life and an approach to the godhead. Hoelderlin in his time has said:

True, the Gods go on living,
But they are over our heads, high in a different world.
Endless there is their work, and little it seems they consider
Whether we live, so much spare us the heavenly ones.
For a frail vessel not always commands the force to contain them,
Only at times can man bear the abundance of Gods.

NOTES

1. "A World of Spiritual Imagery," by Thomas Merton, in *Victor Hammer: An Artist's Testament* (Lexington, Kentucky: The Anvil Press, 1988).
2. *The Forms of Our Letters* by Victor Hammer (Lexington, Kentucky: The Anvil Press, 1988).

Reprinted from *Victor Hammer: An Artist's Testament* (Lexington, Kentucky: The Anvil Press, 1988).

EPICYCLE

Loki the Trickster / Norse

One day, when Thor's wife, Sif, was sleeping, Loki the trickster happened to pass by, and because he was in his usual mischievous mood he took some scissors from his pocket and cut off Sif's beautiful golden hair.

When Thor came home and saw what had happened, he was so full of anger that lightning flashed from his two eyes and the palace trembled beneath his feet.

"I know who has done this," he shouted. "It can be none other than that rascal Loki!" And striding off to the palace of Asgard, he seized Loki by the neck and would have strangled him if Loki had not confessed his deed and promised to restore at once Sif's beauty.

So down he went, deep underground, seeking the dwarfs, the sons of Ivald, who were workers in gold and brass and iron.

"Make me a crown of golden hair that will grow upon the head of Sif and I will give you whatever you ask."

And in no time, the busy dwarfs had fashioned a golden crown for Sif and, in addition, gave to Loki the spear, Gungnir, and the wonderful ship, Skidbladnir.

Loki hurried away to Asgard, boasting of the marvelous treasures he had brought from the sons of Ivald. "No other dwarfs in all the world could have done such work," he boasted.

Now, a dwarf named Brok was standing by, and he called in an angry voice to Loki. "My brother Sindri is a better craftsman than any son of Ivald!"

"If your brother Sindri can make more precious things than these, he can have my head!" said Loki.

"He shall have it, never fear," laughed Brok, and he hurried away to the underworld to tell his brother of the wager.

So the two dwarfs set to work, with Brok blowing the bellows and making the coals a blaze of light and Sindri cleaning a pig's skin and placing it in the furnace.

"Blow till I come back," said Sindri, as he left the smithy to get more coal.

So Brok blew with all his might, taking no notice of a buzzing gadfly that settled on his hand and stung it. And after a while Sindri came back and took out of the furnace a golden boar with bristles that shone in the light.

Then Sindri took a nugget of gold and placed it in the furnace. "Blow for your life!" he said to Brok, and out he went a second time.

The faithful Brok went on with his work and even when the gadfly stung him on the neck, he did not lift his hand from the bellows. And when Sindri came back he took from the fire a golden ring and laid it beside the boar.

Then once more he threw something on the fire. This time it was a lump of iron. "Blow without ceasing," he said to Brok, and he left his brother alone again.

No sooner had he gone than the gadfly settled upon Brok's forehead and stung him so sharply that the blood ran down into both his eyes and he could not see what he was doing. As he raised his hand to brush it away, the bellows ceased to blow. It was at that moment that Sindri returned.

"You have almost spoiled it, brother," he said, as he took from the fire a mighty hammer, still red from the heat of the coals. "The handle is just a trifle short but we cannot alter it now. So take it to Asgard with the boar and the ring and bring me that rascal Loki's head."

IN THE COURTS of Asgard the gods entered and took their thrones and waited to see what would come of the contest. Odin, Thor, and Freya were appointed to judge between Loki and Brok and the gifts which each had brought.

Loki stood forth with the spear, Gungnir, which was known never to miss its mark, and presented it to Odin. The golden hair he handed to Thor, who placed it upon the head of Sif where at once it began to grow. And to Freya he gave the ship Skidbladnir which could sail the sea in any breeze and yet could be folded up like paper and carried in a pocket.

Then he turned and scornfully laughed at Brok. "Can that brother of yours do as well as this? Bring out his paltry trinkets!"

Brok stood before the wondering gods, his treasures in his hands.

"This ring," he said, handing it to Odin, "will cast off, every ninth night, eight other rings as fine as itself. This boar," he declared, giving it to Freya, "will run in the air, on the earth and the sea, and no night will be so dark and gloomy that the shining of these golden bristles will not make it as light as noonday. And this hammer"—he placed the hammer, which was to be known as Mjolner, in the hands of Thor—"shall never fail, no matter how hard the thing it smites. More-

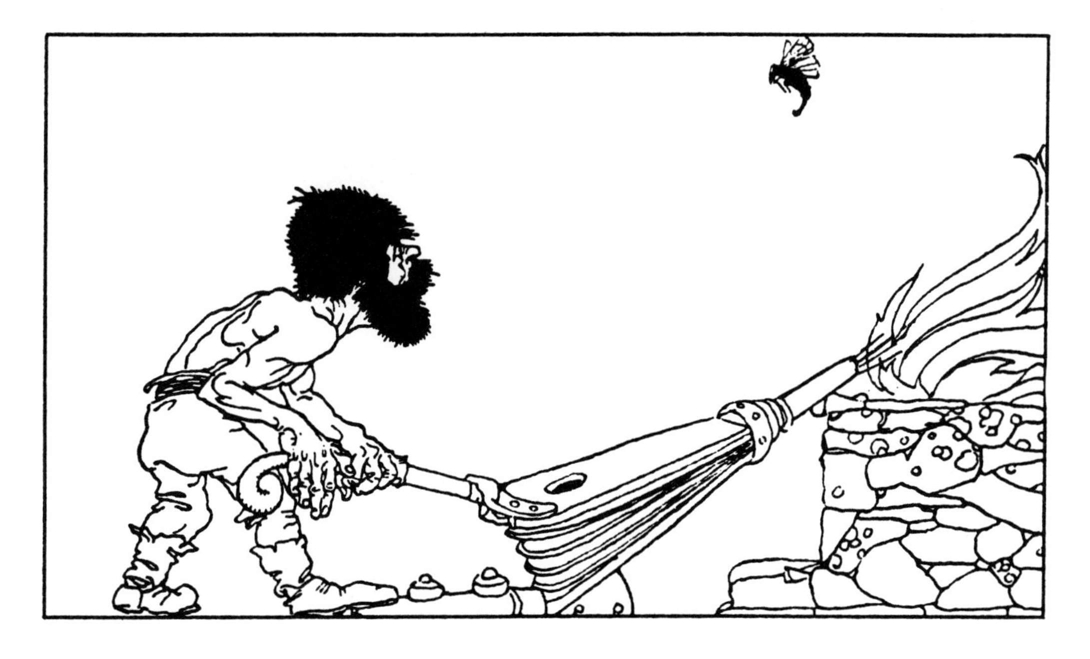

over, however far away you throw it, Mjolner will always return to your hand. You may make it as large or as small as you wish and the only fault to be found with it is the shortness of the handle."

Thor swung the hammer around his head and lightning flashed and flamed in Asgard and thunder rolled through the sky. The other gods surrounded him and passed the hammer from one to the other, declaring that from henceforth it would be their greatest protection against their enemies. "Sindri," they said, "has won the wager."

"Then I shall take him Loki's head," said Brok, drawing his sword.

Loki frowned. He had no intention of paying his debt. "I will give you whatever thing you ask, except my head," he growled.

"Your head or nothing!" answered the dwarf.

"Then take it, if you can," cried Loki. But by the time Brok reached the spot where he had been standing, Loki was far away, for he was wearing his famous shoes that could run through the air or over water.

But Thor, who had even swifter shoes, ran after him and brought him back, for the gods always see to it that promises are kept.

"Well, cut off my head," said the cunning Loki. "But the wager gave you no right to my neck. Do not dare to touch it!"

It was true. And Brok knew it. The head could not be taken without wounding the neck. Sindri had lost his chance of revenge.

But Brok determined to get even with Loki. So he took an awl and a leather thong and sewed the trickster's lips together so that he could do no more boasting.

Thus the dwarfs were satisfied and the gods of Asgard were well content.

—Retold from an old folk tale by P.L. Travers

Reprinted from *A Way of Working*, D.M. Dooling, ed. (New York: Parabola Books, 1986).

Gifts from the Celestial Granary

Marcel Griaule

Blind Ogotemmêli, a Dogon of Africa's Western Sudan, revealed the framework of the Dogon cosmology and religious tradition in a series of thirty-three consecutive conversations with the French ethnologist Marcel Griaule. The following is excerpted from the book Conversations with Ogotemmêli *by Griaule.*

IN THE ROCK-MASS which on the south forms the central square of Upper Ogol, in a small corner of land the smithy is hidden away. It stands on a roughly circular site with low walls of dry stones unmortared and full of openings. Resting on these and supported in the middle by a stake, is a thin layer of branches through which splashes of sunlight fall on the shadows within.

The tools and implements are scattered on the dusty ground without any apparent order. Though the smith has only just left, the smithy looks as if it has been deserted for years. The double bellows, its skins limp, points its two ducts at the dead fire. The anvil like an enormous iron thorn stands on the ground fixed in a beam, which is buried in the earth. Over against it are tongs and some shapeless pieces of iron. The hammer, symbol of the webbed hand of the Spirit of Water, is not to be seen: either it is hidden or the smith has taken it away. Against the wall there is an oven, made of puddled clay, with an opening at the bottom leading to a bowl-shaped outlet above. Close by is a hollow stone from which the water has evaporated.

In the silence and the sunlight all the poverty of the smithy is laid bare. That technique which revolutionized the world, which came down from heaven, and with its tools broke the limbs of the first smith who blew up the fire—a "fragment of the sun"—still exists even in this decay.

"The smithy," said the blind man, "is like a dwelling-house, or again like a person, whose head is the oven and his two arms the bellows with its two ducts."

In the primal field, in which the flying granary landed, the smithy was erected on the north side at the edge of the land which was to be cleared. That is why today smithies are always erected on the north side of the central square, which itself is always to the north of the village.

"You can see," said Ogotemmêli, turning his head to one side, "you can see over the wall."

The central square of Lower Ogol was indeed there behind the ruined granary of the backyard on the left. The high central rock, the square millstone of the council house, the cube-shaped stone known as the "Stone of the Brave" and, on the left, facing full north, a smithy sister to that of Upper Ogol, were all clearly to be seen.

But here all was according to rule, whereas in the other village the plan of the building was completely different.

"At first," said Ogotemmêli, "the smith did not have all the tools that he has today. He had no hafted hammer, no file, and no tongs. The red-hot iron was held in the bare hand; and that is something one can still see today, when the smiths come together for funerals. As they chant the dirges for the dead, they pick up red-hot iron in their hands in memory of the practice of the first smiths."

THE CHIEF TOOL, he went on to say, is the hammer. The celestial granary[1] was a hammer; and everybody believes that it was in this hammer that the seeds came down from heaven. The hammer is the webbed hand of the Water Spirit. The arm is the cone-shaped handle, and the hand itself is the four-sided face of the tool with which it strikes.

The hammer is also the whole body of the Water Spirit, the male Great Nummo[2] in heaven. Two of the opposite sides are his arms, and the other two his back and chest. The cone-shaped handle is the serpent's tail in which the lower part of his body ends.

The anvil is something like the implement reapers use; it is the female form of the hammer, and represents the female Great Nummo. The slab at the top is very narrow but rectangular, and it ends in a blunt point. There is often a small hole at this lower end, reminiscent of the part played by the hammer, that is by the granary, in the organization of the world, when its interior, symbolized by this hole, was full of organs and seeds.

The beam in which the anvil is embedded is made of a medium-sized tree-trunk about a cubit in length, roughly squared. It is sunk in the earth in a line north-south, as all men's beds should lie.

The wood of the anvil is the bed of the two great Water Spirits. When the hammer strikes the iron, the two come together.

The two earthenware pots of the bellows are modelled in clay, with which wool from a white sheep is mixed. This addition gives greater cohesion to the material, which is not baked but dried slowly in the air. The sheep's wool is a symbol of the celestial Ram, avatar of the Nummo.

The two spherical pots symbolize the sun, being of the same shape, while the wool in their clay comes from the fleece of the Spirit, which is of copper, the sun's excrement. They are also associated with that luminary by the skins which cover them, and by means of which air is conveyed to the fire. The other, which the smith in flight brandished over his head, had already acquired a fiery quality from contact with its fellow-skin, and was able to sustain unscathed the discharge of the thunderbolts.

The ducts of dry earth which connect the pots with the fire-grate afford a passage for the air expelled by the skins; and this air is a breath of the sun, and so animates the fire.

FROM THE HOLLOW stone the smith draws water with a stick, with which to damp down the fire. The Nummo is in this puddle as in all water, and he moved in it by swimming, his movements following the rhythm of the blows on the anvil and the alternating puffs of the bellows.

"The smith," said Ogotemmêli,

Pottery was born in the smithy.

"in striking the anvil is asking the earth to restore to him the strength of which he had formerly emptied himself."

For, when the smith of the celestial granary came down to the defiled earth, he put into it a great portion of his own pure strength, depriving himself in order to give the soil a life-force favorable to the great work he was about to do.

As a result he and his descendants became endowed with a special quality, which made them different from men, whether "impure" *(puru)* or "living" *(omo)* or "white" *(pili)*.

The "impure" are the descendants of the first initiates of the Great Mask, the upholders of the spiritual principles of the first dead man; the "living" are the other Dogon; the "whites" are people like shoemakers, minstrels, and men of the various peoples dwelling in the plains.

The characteristic feature of the smiths is a diminished life-force, which removes them from the category of the "living." But this diminishment is not like the effect of death, which separates them also from the "impure." Nor are they comparable to the "whites," for these are insensitive to certain sources of impurity. Though they have, like other people, individual altars for both head and body *(kutogolo, djabyé),* they have to be constantly engaged on some other means of self-support; and this is provided for them by the exercise of their craft.

"By striking the anvil," said Ogotemmêli, "they get back from the earth some of the life-force they gave it. Their blows recover it."

But blows on the iron must be dealt by day. The smith's work is day labor, no doubt because the smithy fire, being a fragment of the sun, could not shine at night. That is why it is forbidden, not only for smiths but for everybody, to strike blows on iron or stone or earth in the nighttime. No blow of hammer or tap of pestle should be heard, whether loud or soft, in the silent hours. To strike blows at night would destroy the effect of the blows struck by day. It would mean the rejection of all that had been gained, so that the smith would lose whatever he had recovered during the day of the life-force of which he formerly divested himself.

The fines inflicted on those who strike blows by night are used to provide victims for the foundation altar of the village, which in former times was erected above a man buried standing, who had offered his strength and his body for the stability of the human settlement on the new earth.

THUS WAS RESTORED the broken order of that relationship between the earth and the one who emptied himself to purify it and to enable men to pursue their life-giving labors.

In the primal field the smith had assigned to his own family one of the eight sectors marked out around the point of impact of the granary. But what he was concerned to do was merely to establish his right to the produce from it, for he was not at any time to cultivate it himself.

His part is to forge the implements of cultivation, but never to use them with his own hand; the hoes that he makes are for the men of the seven other families, and it is for them in return to supply him with food. So we see how, every year at harvest-time, the smith leaves his forge and goes about the country to collect the grain from the plots which the implements of his forging have worked. He knows all the fields which owe him tribute: there is nothing he does not know about their growth and their maturity.

So it is that, when the sweating peasant opens up to the sunlight the soil which lay in the shade of the growing corn, and reaps the last ear, he sees seated at the edge of the field, watching him open-mouthed and in silence, the smith.

POTTERY WAS BORN in the smithy. The smith's wife was drying in the sun a pot which she had modeled like one of the spheres of the bellows; but, finding it did not harden quickly enough, she put it near the fire. She then discovered that the clay was baking and becoming hard, and so she got into the habit of putting the pots she modeled by the fire.

She worked on a small square mat woven with eighty strings on a warp of the same number. First she made a rough model shaped like a section of an inverted cone, into which she threw with considerable force a round pebble, which made a bed for itself in the clay, and this became larger and larger until finally it took

In molding the clay the woman is imitating the work of God.

the shape of a sphere. When the inside surface of the clay was pressed it took the pattern of the mat.

Women today copy the processes of the mythical potteress; but the craft is no longer the prerogative of the wives of smiths. Any woman can be a potter, if she wishes.

"The mat," said Ogotemmêli, "on which the woman works, is a symbol of that of the first human couple. The craft of pottery is like a person on a mat. In molding the clay the woman is imitating the work of God, when he modeled the earth and the first couple. She is creating a being, and the round pot is like a head resting on the mat, a head or a womb. A pot without ornament symbolizes a man, a pot with two small breasts a woman."

Ogotemmêli had before him one of the pots used for brewing millet-beer. He passed his hand over its belly as he spoke, to feel the pattern imprinted on it.

"The mat on which the potter works has eighty threads one way and eighty threads the other. It is woven like one square of the pall that covers the dead, but with fibers of baobab instead of cotton."

BAOBAB FIBERS are much used among the Dogon for cords and plaited objects of all kinds. One sees rings a couple of cubits deep round the trunks of trees from which the bark has been torn.

"This fiber-plaiting is men's work and resembles weaving. The best work is done in Banani. Patterns made on pots in this way make one think one has one's mat with one for repose wherever one goes."

"And what," Ogotemmêli was asked, "of the pebble with which the clay is struck?"

"The stone," was the reply, "which the woman rolls in the clay is the symbol of the food which will be cooked in the pot."

"How was meat cooked before there were clay pots?"

"Before pottery was invented," said Ogotemmêli, "men ate their meat raw." In an earlier conversation he had compared the moon to a pot heated a quarter at a time. This symbol has another application.

"Before the clay has been baked," he went on to explain, "the open end of the pot recalls the circumference of the moon. After the baking it represents the circumference of the sun. That is intelligible enough," he added, "for one must suppose the moon is less completely cooked than the sun."

So a humble pot is an epitome of the universe, with its own mat on its surface.

NOTES

1. Symbol of the world system.
2. The original twin ancestors of mankind.

Excerpted from *Conversations with Ogotemmêli: An Introduction to Dogon Religious Ideas* (London: Oxford University Press, 1965).

Close to the Earth

Gladys Remde

POTTERY IS a primal craft. It has to do with earthy elements acted on by water, air, and fire. Clay itself is primal stuff, formed from rock ground into dust over an immense time span. Steeped in water and organic residues, it has a unique structure. Hexagonal platelets are layered in ionically charged water, which holds the platelets together and also cushions them, giving clay its well-known qualities of cohesiveness and plasticity.

When it is dried and burned in fire, the clay pot, so reversible to dust in its raw state, turns back to rock and lasts as long. Early civilizations are identified by shards of their pottery.

People needed containers. Maybe they wove baskets of reeds. Maybe a woman daubed clay into a basket to make it watertight, then put it on the fire. Maybe the basket burned away, leaving its imprint on a permanent container, a fired pottery bowl. Such ancient bowls have been found.

Pottery reflects its intimacy with the people who form and use it. The sensitive clay invites the hand to shape it. No tool is needed, just the touch of hands and fingers rolling, pressing, turning, smoothing, guided by the potter's instinct for hollowness. The bowl fits the cupped hands. Maybe the potter needs a cooking pot, a storage jar, a jug. She forms them like the shell of a body. They have a foot, belly, shoulder, neck, mouth, lip.

Native people still make pottery completely by hand, perhaps with a few natural tools, a piece of gourd, a shell, a stone. They dig the clay, grind the colors, gather fuel for the fire. With immense patience they make their pots, referring again and again to an inner sense of structure, roundness, and beautiful curve. The quiet satisfaction in working this way, close to the earth, can be seen in their faces.

Folk potters once provided for the needs of village households. They worked at home or perhaps in a small shared cottage industry. Their potter's wheel was a highly personal machine which they could "play" like a musical instrument, enhancing and amplifying their work. Their pots were simple and unaffected, made with a human touch for human use—and sold directly to the user.

Today technology takes precedence. Factory-made goods are scarcely touched by human hands. There is no contact between maker and user. In fact, is there a human maker? Perhaps there is a mold maker in the factory, but many mechanized processes have intervened before the piece is finished. Maybe a worker has painted a few brush strokes on the piece, which is one of thousands. Once could say that the factory itself is an enormous machine, and the workers, assigned to repetitive tasks with no concept of the whole, are replaceable parts of the machine.

The way the fire affects the clay is the great mystery of the craft.

IT IS NOT surprising that crafts are enjoying a resurgence. Potters no longer supply common utensils. Yet there is a place for their way of working. Man feels deprived in a world ruled by technology. He hungers for contact with the fundamentals of life. His eye searches for things made with human care; his hand yearns to touch and hold the handmade. The potter can help to fill these needs.

Working with clay is working close to the earth, not just because clay is earth, but because one must continually be aware of the "earthly" processes that affect the clay: the way water lubricates, softens, expands it; the way air dries, shrinks, and hardens it; the way the stony elements of raw glaze adhere to it; the way fire transforms it. From the very beginning, one needs to visualize these changes.

The potter's wheel has been an integral part of the craft for so long that one does not think of it as a machine. It is a simple machine, yet it changes very much the way the potter relates to her work. The wheel introduces the law of centrifugal force and puts new demands on the potter. She must attune herself to the action of this law.

First she must prepare the clay so it is even and free of air pockets. She kneads or "wedges" it with a rhythmic motion of her whole body. Now she throws the lump of clay onto the wheelhead, wets it and spins it fast, enclosing the resisting, thumping mass in her hands as she leans strongly into it, employing all the weight and muscle of her body. If she is firm and centered in herself, the clay becomes centered; a smooth mound, spinning around the still axis of the wheel. She thrusts wet thumbs into the center, opens it, and, with a few deft motions, draws up a thin-walled cylinder. As the solid mass becomes hollow, it takes on a kind of life, breathes, and has a voice. (If you sing into it, it will resonate to its own note.)

Watching a pot being shaped on the wheel seems like magic. The wet clay appears to be alive, it changes

shape so smoothly, so quickly, the cylinder rounding into an ample curve, narrowing to a thin neck, opening into a finely articulated lip. Behind the magic is the subtlety of the potter's skill, her attention to the varying speeds and pressures needed, her delicacy of touch as the thin wall rises, softens, and becomes more and more sensitive to the forces acting on it. Leaning on the air in defiance of gravity, the wet clay reaches its limit of tolerance. Gently the wheel is brought to a stop.

THE WAY THE FIRE affects the clay is the great mystery of the craft. The potter knows she must light a tiny flame and increase it ever so slowly so as not to shock the clay's fragile rawness; she knows she must ease the fire past the red heat that warns of a sudden crystalline expansion; she knows when to feed air to the flame and when to starve it so it will steal the oxides from the clay and glazes, reversing their colors; she knows when, at the searing height of the fire, the glowing, shimmering shapes have said, "Enough! Enough!" She knows all this without seeing what goes on in the kiln, except through a tiny peephole. Vicariously she enters the kiln and visits her burning wares.

The moment of opening the kiln is a moment of suspense. The potter, having done her best, must bow to the forces of nature. Have earth and water, air, and fire danced together? Or have they fought and clashed? For better or worse the fire has done its work. The clay is rock, the glazes an alchemical blend of colors and textures. The potter accepts her pieces. Maybe just one is especially beautiful. Maybe not. Maybe next time.

She walks a thin line between success and failure. There are many steps in the craft, many elements to be brought into right relationship. Each step must be given close care and attention. Each step must be related to the whole. There are failures along the way, so many that the potter becomes inured to them. She simply starts again.

A POTTER is said to need brains in her fingers and in her "potter's thumb." She also needs her head brain to solve never-ending problems that arise from the complexity of the craft. Many subtle variables keep her mind alert and flexible. She is continually faced with the "why" as well as the "how" as she moves from one step of the process to another. The process of learning never stops. As Chaucer put it: "The lyf so short, the crafte so long to lerne" (*Parlement of Foules*).

All this is true if a potter follows the traditional way, if she herself takes responsibility for the essential steps of the process. In meeting the demands of the craft, she develops an inner strength that can meet the demands of life. At the same time she feels her place in relation to natural forces greater than herself.

In the Old Testament, pottery is used as an example of man's relationship to God. In Jeremiah 18:3-6, the Lord tells the prophet to go to the potter's house.

Then I went down to the potter's house, and, behold, he wrought a work on the wheels. And the vessel that he made of clay was marred in the hand of the potter: so he made it again another vessel, as seemed good to the potter to make it. Then the word of the Lord came to me, saying, O house of Israel, cannot I do with you as this potter? saith the Lord. Behold, as the clay is in the potter's hand, so are ye in mine hand, O house of Israel.

Both the clay and the creator of pots are subject to the laws of the Creator.

Although clay is responsive and flexible, it cannot be forced against its nature. The potter dreams of beautiful shapes and colors. And one needs to dream. But in the actual making, one learns that both the clay and the creator of pots are subject to the laws of the Creator. One may not be able to define these laws but encounters them repeatedly in trying to make a vision real. The clay will do one's will only within the limits of these laws.

It is said that clay has a memory. It easily accepts the marks of hand or tool. It shows the character and state of its maker. The potter's struggle, feeling, skill, attention (or lack of it), are reflected there. This human element is an essential part of the potter's craft. When it is missing or minimized, pottery becomes dull and lifeless or cheap and garish.

When the potter learns to listen, both to her own essential nature and to the nature of the clay, she begins to feel a oneness between herself and the clay. Opening to this feeling, she discovers a new source of creativity. It is as if something were being created not by her, but through her. It is then that she feels a new joy, a new love for her work. It is then that a piece may appear that has an indefinable quality of beauty. It stands out from all the others. Seeing it, touching it, awakens feeling in the user.

This is the exchange that is made possible by the real craft of pottery. •

Writing with Light

Paul Caponigro

Photographs by the Author

Born of the earth,
Struck by the fire of light,
Shaped by the waters of chemistry
And reflected through the shimmering
mirror
Of lens and air,
Grains of intently polished silver
Awaken the mother's sleeping child
In the land of light
And give now reflections of that womb
From which was derived the original dark
mirror.

DURING THE 1830s, a child of light appeared on the horizon. Helios, the Sun, consorted as light with the salts and silvers of Mother Earth, producing a child then known as heliography, and now as photography, or writing with light. A certain excitement stirred in the masses whose hands, once used for crafting, no longer had that function, but could have it again, through this new process. One did not need a university degree or a long apprenticeship with a master in order to make these images etched with light.

Following the invention of photography, it was only a matter of time

St. Mac Dara's Church, Ireland

Silver metal is being crafted in an entirely different manner.

---

before individuals saw its potential for being an effective medium of creative expression and realized that artists with maturity of vision could impart heart through this new machine and its chemical partners. Photography's status as an "art" remained somewhat suspect, however, because it was a relatively easy craft to learn in comparison to painting, music, and sculpture. The questions remained: Who or what was behind the final statement of the work? Were photographers, with their palettes of dark and light silver tones, sufficiently inspired to match the best works of painters with their palettes of primary colors, or the power of musicians working from tonal scales and rhythms?

In earlier times, metals were extracted from earth and placed in the hands of craftsmen for purposeful shaping. Now in this age of technology, silver metal is being crafted in an entirely different manner through photography's blending of light and chemical solutions. This process enables the photographer to depict highly detailed and lifelike objects or landscapes by etching and shaping the silver within emulsions. These elements are gifts from sun and earth, and, when treated with appropriate reverence, they provide a palette as full of potential as that of any artistic medium.

My own methods of working with photographic materials are not significantly different from the basic techniques of the past seventy-five years, but I attempt to use and appreciate the refinements of the process that have been made in recent years. My method differs from those of the past mainly in that I try to prevent the excessive intrusion of intellectual preconceived notions concerning final results. I have no special techniques of my own for making negatives or prints: I simply work hard using already known and published methods. It seems better to suggest to others that they embark on their own journeys and learn how to do something through the direct experience of trial and error.

Experimenting with new materials, tools, or techniques requires time. This testing can be a preparation for craft, as well as a meditation on it. Rather than a drudgery or inconvenience, it can be an opportunity to explore the unique potential locked in the emulsions. Though some photographers hire an assistant to process film and print for them, others go deeper into the process by acquainting themselves intimately with the tones, color, and scale of films, papers, and developers. Simple photographic step wedges of tone, ranging from dark to light, created through the agencies of time, light, and chemicals, can exhibit a unique beauty; one can respond to them with far more feeling and sensitivity than to the results of intricate,

St. Cronan Church, Ireland

The process should involve not just the chemical but also the alchemical.

---

sensitometric measurements of time and light.

I believe the process should involve not just the chemical but also the alchemical, linking the photographic tradition to the greater tradition of calling forth a higher consciousness. In the end, tools and materials must allow access to the inner realm of awareness which alone is capable of transcending preconceptions. Techniques are essential, but their use is in assisting to liberate an attention that is above the intellect. This attention can be kept alive during the entire process, enabling the photographer to make more pertinent decisions and discoveries to obtain better results.

In my own work, I make a distinction between my physical techniques and a deeper craft; I see the latter as my "inner technique." Excessive preoccupation with outer technique can result in making a print that dazzles the mind with a brilliant combination of materials, but the other approach allows one to combine many separate elements, creating a print that nourishes not only the mind but the spirit as well. The total process involves both the shaping of photo emulsions and the shaping of internal attitudes; and the goal is to keep the techniques in the service of that which is beyond the ego.

FOR A CRAFTSMAN, it is important to gather and use the materials lovingly, and this attitude allows the materials and the technique to teach one their ways. Along with the inner attitudes, the art of waiting needs to be cultivated. Silence is a tool of the intuitive realm, the vehicle of inspiration, just as readiness is the vehicle of physical techniques. Standing in readiness for any possibility allows recognition of outer conditions that might serve one's deeper intent. Recognition is the ambassador of seeing.

Nothing is truly dead, even within the various levels of earth substance; stones simply breathe too quietly and slowly for their breath to be perceptible. In a craft, it is often the attitude of the individual working with the material—not the materials themselves—that is really dead or comatose. Can fires be kindled under these cold attitudes to enliven the working process, and to impart depth and warmth to it?

Through receptivity and communion, one can open to a higher consciousness, remembering that this quiet inner attention is a most precious energy which can be used throughout the total process. Recording the light of the outer subject can be linked with gaining access to one's inner light. This reciprocity can also be part of the printmaking process, where the print surface is the ground for transpositions of light and revelation.

Reefert Church, Ireland

The task of the photographer is to put beauty of image into the world through silver prints.

Although earlier work and traditions can be used as a point of departure, one's work needs to be dissociated sufficiently from the known—not by intentional avoidance, exaggerated divergence, or forced originality, but according to the artist's ability to contact his or her own source. This contact is made by learning to surrender to the subject and to one's inspiration. Is it more important to avoid sameness of subject, as many in the current art world seem to think, or to see that all life is one great cathedral in which anyone, regardless of time or place, is free to worship? Perhaps what is necessary is one's own relation to the subject: a loving attention which imbues any work with a nourishing substance.

True art is produced by means of an "intelligence of love," a love that makes the gymnastics of the ego pale by comparison. This exists apart from emotional agreements between individuals, immature bargaining, or mere chemical affinities. This higher love penetrates and feeds all dimensions of being; it does not meander through sentimentality or extol cleverness as does the intellect, but exudes a quiet, radiant, and elevating substance. This intelligence of love derives from a deeper source and never becomes bound to a personality or its work. It is not a jealous lover, but a sustainer of something higher. Works of art that have been created from this source have unfailingly nourished, for such art embodies a profound mystery.

ONE OF THE most important aspects of the process of making negatives or prints is maintaining enough distance and stillness to allow a pristine experience to pass through the instruments to the inner eye. If one can cast a quiet glance on the forms and visual rhythms of earth and sky before making exposure on film, the compositions will not be forced or fabricated, will not pit forms or masses of light and dark indiscriminately against one another in the name of design or just to make something "interesting." Instead, one senses proportions within the subject: a qualitative experience that is emotionally apprehended, rather than mentally calculated.

The task of a photographer is to put beauty of image into the world through silver prints. While pursuing this activity, it is possible to encounter truth, since beauty and ugliness are intimately connected to truth. The necessary striving is to express nature's subtle realms, however elusive, and to photograph for the simple pleasure of the creative act; to continue to discover the transformations occurring through the agents of light, lens, and chemistry, as well as to divine the art of that language unique to the materials of photography; to use the eye as the ear would hear music; and to try to grasp the silver voice of the print. ●

Tournous Abbey, France

The Master in the Stone

AN INTERVIEW WITH ALAN BIRD

Photographs by Lee B. Ewing

Walking into the quiet hugeness of the nave of the Cathedral of St. John the Divine, on New York City's Upper West Side, one cannot help but be moved by the grandeur and majesty of an incomplete master-work-in-progress. The second largest church in the world (only St. Peter's in Rome is bigger), the cathedral remains unfinished today, some ninety-nine years after the cornerstone was laid in 1892. The building was first conceived as Romanesque, with Byzantine/Islamic overtones, but the plan was changed to traditional Gothic by architect Ralph Adams Cram in 1911.

The cathedral rose slowly—part by part: the crypt, the outside columns, the choir, the transept, the long central nave area. The west wall, with its monumental rose window, was completed in 1933. A week-long celebration to honor the official opening of the cathedral in late 1941 ended the day before the attack on Pearl Harbor: the world war that ensued caused the halt of all construction on the building, a hiatus that lasted until 1978, when Master Builder James Bambridge was brought over from England to begin training neighborhood youths as apprentice stone-masons so that the final phase of construction—the southwest and northwest towers—could begin.

In 1980, Alan Bird came from Wells Cathedral in England to join the project. Bird's status in masonry is Clerk of the Works, which he says means he's "the guy in charge of everything relating to fabrication, sort of like chief cook and bottle washer." PARABOLA*'s co-editors, Ellen Draper and Rob Baker, accompanied by writer Marvin Barrett (a longtime friend of both the cathedral and the magazine, of which he is a contributing editor), spoke to Bird recently in the Cathedral House office of the Very Reverend James Parks Morton, Dean of the Cathedral and a main force behind the ongoing construction and completion of the awe-inspiring space.*

—The Editors

Parabola: In exploring the question of "Craft," we've become quite interested in how craft can transform the material, the craftsman, and even the larger community. In the case of medieval stonemasons, this community included both their own workers' guild and the congregation of the cathedral on which they were working. Do these various transformations still take place today?

Alan Bird: If I start off by telling you a bit about myself as a third-generation craftsman, and the way I feel about my particular craft, that may give some insights into what craftsmen and -women feel. So let me begin by saying that I started back in England in 1967. I was first apprenticed at Wells Cathedral. My grandfather was a craftsman; he was a trained wheelwright, but he later adapted to stone building and stone cutting. My father also was in the stone trade, and then I took up the tools in 1967. I also had an uncle who worked on Bath Abbey.

I don't really know what draws people—what drew *me*—to stone. We always say, you know, you have stone dust in the blood. But there's something that drew me, at a really young age. Maybe it was because it was in the family; maybe it's something within. But I've now spent the last twenty-five years working in stone, at two cathedrals, the one in England and the one here. I've been here eleven years. Craft, of course, is not everything, but yet it is.

P: This seems to be what we're really finding about craft in its truest sense: that it always has this attraction that can't really be pinned down—this power or hold over the craftsman that links him to the work in a very intimate way.

AB: I think the big thing that draws you is what it does to people, how they feel. Especially here. The cultural aspect of craft: we've been training young Americans from Harlem who have not had the opportunity of a great education. So I've gone back to square one and started teaching basic math and simple reading, so that they can understand what they're cutting, what they're doing. I think you start to get that feeling that people grow, and as they grow in skill, they also grow within themselves. The cathedral is a great place to nurture that.

P: What is required to be a good stonemason?

AB: You've got to have a lot of patience, with yourself as well as the material you're using. You don't come to hand-and-eye coordination easily: the feeling that you have, you must put in that stone. You're only going to get out of the stone what you put in it. If you have a lot of anger on a particular day, that will reflect in your work. Every stroke that you make with the chisel is a reflection of how you're feeling at that particular moment. If you're feeling good, then the work will be light and will flow. You can read how a person is by the work they're doing. You begin to understand that this is not just another job, that there is a lot more to it. You've got your character, your identity stamped all over that, whether you want it or not. And most people really want it.

Each chisel mark has a little variation. Each student or craftsperson will hold the tool at a little different angle. His identity is all over that piece of stone—whether it's a piece of flat ashlar or whether it's an ornate piece of gothic stiff leaf.

A good craftsperson can read another person's work. I think that's why back in medieval times the really top craftspeople never put their mason's mark on the stone. They didn't need to: the work spoke for itself. Anybody could look at that work and say who cut what.

P: So is individuality supposed to show through?

AB: Absolutely. But if you take it to the next stage—actually trying to complete a tower, as we are here—you have to bring all that individuality, the character of each person, and you mold that, you put that into a tower. That's what makes that tower come to life, which is what handcraft is about. It's going to rise above the Hudson River, and it should dance before your eyes. I think the rest of this cathedral—and maybe I shouldn't say this—but it seems very mechanical for me. If I look at all the granite on the exterior, it's all been bush-hammered, it's all of a lifeless, mechanical appearance. Every arris is so sharp and straight. It's all been done on planing machines. And the little quirks, the little inadequacies are missing: the life is not there.

I think you will see, eventually, when our tower is let out of jail—I always think of it as entrapped, because it's encased in scaffolding at the moment—when that is finally taken away, you will really see the life that's gone into building the tower that we're doing now.

P: Have you had the experience of seeing your work come out of this long imprisonment? All craftspersons go through a process of preparation and execution, but yours seems much longer than, say, that of a potter or weaver or metalworker.

AB: When I was at Wells, I spent thirteen years there, and a lot of that work was on the west facade, on the restoration, and when I left in 1980, it was still entrapped in scaffolding. So after thirteen years, I hadn't seen any of my work through fruition. It took me six years here before I could return. It was quite an experience to walk up to the west front and see the work out of jail, so to speak. And I think it really sank in then, the realization of what handwork means: the intensity and the concentration that my colleagues and I had put in during those thirteen years.

P: But how do you avoid having this individuality turn into ego, which can be very counterproductive in a craft?

AB: I don't think you can completely avoid it: you have to mold it. Artisans in general are a very fickle bunch, very temperamental. I think that basically my job is to try to get everybody to work within a theme, which is Gothic. But you don't want to kill the individuality, the design, the creativity that they have in their minds. So what I like to do—and I believe they did the same thing back in medieval times—is to allow that creativity, those ideas, to come through the leaf work. For instance, one of the apprentices was doing a corbel out over Amsterdam Avenue on the southwest corner, where there was all this Gothic stiff leaf, and he carved a face with an excruciating look on it, with fingers in its ears, because of the traffic noise below. Now that was his idea: that was what he wanted to do on that particular part of the tower. I encourage that.

P: How would you describe the difference between the work you did as an apprentice on Wells Cathedral and the work here?

AB: The main difference is in the people. Obviously, Wells Cathedral itself is much smaller, and the two cities are very different in size as well. But the main thing is the people. When I was back in England, I was mostly

dealing with youngsters, from sixteen to twenty-one, because you can't be an apprentice after you are twenty-one in England, by law. Here, I'm dealing with people who already have a lot of responsibility, so they tend to be very thoughtful, very sincere about what they're doing. Whereas youngsters back there were interested in young girls and fast motorbikes, and it was hard to get them to concentrate on the skill and the long-term aspect. Very few youngsters tend to look at the long-term view.

This craft is very long-term. I've been doing it twenty-five years and I still feel I'm an apprentice. I worked with a gentleman in England who spent fifty-two years of his life on one building. His statement to me was: There's only one master and you're looking at it. And that was the piece of stone. That's the master. If anyone—you talk about ego!—if anyone thinks that he is master of his craft, then he's kidding himself. We're all apprentices; I think this is a lifetime apprenticeship.

P: Doesn't this apprenticeship—this grounding in technique—keep ego from taking over too much? Isn't there a rather complicated language you have to learn?

AB: Yes, you do. And also, there comes a bond with one another, too. There's that mutual respect. One grows in craft, and one achieves certain standards and goals, regarding the differences in the carving or cutting or whatever one is following. That starts to form *mutually*, and it forms very quickly.

P: How long does it really take you to learn the basic tools and concepts of your trade? Or do you ever?

AB: To be able to control fully every tool on every piece of stone is, I think, tantamount to impossible. Each stone is formed a little differently. One's softer, one's harder. You have to be able to understand and read each stone. So if you've got that sort of whiteness, when the matrix tightens, you know your stroke has to be a little firmer, to cut that. And as you go to the softer part, you have to lighten your stroke. There's always a nice flow to the work. You're always reading the color and the difference in the makeup of the stone that you're cutting: that's all going through your mind. It's sort of eye-hand coordination with the mind. It's a three-way triangulation here that you're talking about. Reading stone is very important, and also listening to stone. The ring of that chisel, as it comes off.

You know, before, in England, a lot of the quarries were almost worked out—what we call played out—because the old people really knew their stone: they took all of that stone. We were dealing with second-class stone. And a little pocket in the quarry of really good quality stone was very hard to come by. Another knack that the old people had: they knew how to go out and look at a four- to ten-ton block and see all the inadequacies. And one of the techniques they used was ringing it. They would take a big chisel, tip it upside down, and pop it across the surface: ding, ding, ding, DUM. Once you heard that really dull sound, you knew that there was a natural fault in there—what we call cricks—so you weren't going to buy that block of stone.

Listening to stone is very important—even as you cut. When you're working on a ten-ton block, you're not going to hear every little imperfection. You may have a pretty solid piece of stone, but as you get into it, as you're carving into it, you can come across little pockets that are not of the same nature. So as you cut, the sweetness of the sound of that chisel as it cuts is all language to the mason, and he's reading that as it comes off. He has to know, as soon as he hears that little sound, that something's not quite right. That will make him check, stop, look at what's happening.

When you're going through as an apprentice, you're learning all these things as you go. That takes time: and each stone is a law unto itself. You're not going to learn all these things overnight.

The other thing is to have patience with oneself. You're not going to create some wonderful piece of sculpture or carving in a matter of a few years; you're just not going to do it. This is an age-old craft. It takes ages to perfect. And I don't think anyone every really perfects it.

P: Do your apprentices live together here?

AB: We have one building where we have about eight people living together.

P: Is that important?

AB: Yes, but I feel working here on the grounds is equally important. Because you get the feeling of the building, of what's going on in the building. That's very important, too: the

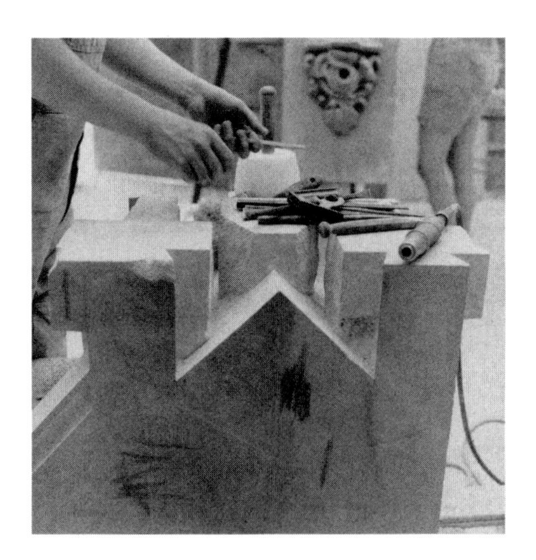

cathedral itself, and the social programs that are going on within it. That's very important to getting the feeling of what it takes to be a stone mason. Because you have to have that kind of—how can I describe it?—compassion, perhaps, for people.

Today life to me is like conveyor belts, especially here in New York—and you'd better run to keep up. Sometimes we're not as compassionate with one another as I feel we should be. I think, to go back to the craft, that you can't be like that in this craft. You've got to give people time. Especially if, maybe, they've neglected their education or if it's been interrupted, or substandard or whatever. Whatever the problems are. And I think the cathedral sort of suggests the understanding that we need to help the community. We need to give individuals the time to absorb what it takes to even get close to being a master mason. (I hate the term master mason, by the way. It's an age-old legal term, master mason. I don't think I've ever met one yet. But maybe a head mason or something like that.) You need to give the person that time.

And the persons themselves have to allow themselves the time. It's very easy to get frustrated with oneself, especially when you're first starting out, because you're not going to see the results. We have an obligation to the masons of the old days. This cathedral's never been finished; it was started in 1892. We have an obligation to continue their dream—to try and get it to the next stage. We have a two-fold commitment, in a way, to continue the craft, to continue this cathedral, for the dream that the masons before had—and a commitment to the next generation. We have to pass on the skills that we have, with the hope that they can be enhanced, and maybe even restored. I'm sure the skills I have in my hands today are not of the same high degree as those of masons of years past, because so much has been lost. We've let the old skills drop—because of the almighty god of chasing after what we call progress. But our buildings today do not reflect progress. Something that was built as Wells was, eight hundred years ago, still stands today and is magnificent and glorious, and everybody from all over the world comes to see it. But people build things here in Manhattan that maybe will last fifty years. I don't call that progress.

I want my stone that I'm cutting today to last for a thousand years. I look at it that way, and I want to be able to put the time into that. A lot of people say to me, well, your stone's going to go 250 feet in the air. Who on earth is going to see it? So I say, well, let's look at a James Bond movie, and he's got this jet-pack on his back. OK? Maybe ten years down the road from now, people are going to have jet-packs and they're going to go up and say, let's go and see what Alan Bird did on that little piece of stone up there. Let's go and see the mistakes he made. We've got to bear all that in mind.

P: Perhaps in the same way that a craftsman's mastering his craft is never finished, a cathedral is never finished either.

AB: Never. I don't think a cathedral's work is ever done. Whether it's on the social side—where obviously it could never be done—or the building, which reflects that. And I think that comes back to the craft: the building, in time, is always going to need help. Wells has been there for eight hundred years, yes. Has it deteriorated? Yes. Do we need to maintain it and keep the beauty? Yes. Is it worth while? Yes. I think people get a lot—that their lives are enriched through working with their hands in craft, they feel good about themselves and about their colleagues, about other people. It teaches so much about having time for one another—about what is good, what is right, what is stable. That's what's missing in life today among a lot of young people that I've worked with here. The one thing they don't have is that piece of stone in their life. Nothing is stable. A lot of my guys have been abandoned. There's not a mother-father situation. There's not the trust. But stone teaches all these things.

P: Most people who work in New York City seem to be almost completely separated from what they do. They get a job, they stumble through it in a daze, they change jobs all the time. There's no real commitment, no real feeling of responsibility, or duty. And often there's no connection with anyone else they work with, there's no sense of any sort of higher purpose.

AB: Absolutely. My guys, at first, when they did something wrong and I shouted at them, which I did quite often, they expected to be abandoned immediately. I had to learn that here in New York, if you make a mistake, you're abandoned, you're gone, you're history. So that was what I had to learn: to have the kind of extra patience that I needed to understand that, not just the craft, but the people—to understand their emotions, what they were going through, to get them to the point where they can come in the door and say, "Yes, I belong here; this is my place of work, this is my second home. I feel comfortable here."

It took a long time for some of the guys to come to me and say that they can't read, for example, to say: "Well, wait a minute. You're doing all this with me and explaining things, but I really can't read what you're writing down here." So, you have to

understand, you have to have the compassion, the feeling. And the cathedral environment allows that.

P: So the teacher learns as well in this apprenticeship.

AB: The teacher is constantly learning from the pupil. If he doesn't, then he is not open enough. He has to be aware of that, he has to bear it in mind. It's a never-ending learning process.

P: Do most of your apprentices finish?

AB: No. Unfortunately. I would like to say yes. But no. It's a tremendous barrier: the time factor, adjusting the concept of time. Four years is a very long time to these guys. Four years for them is a very big achievement. They've probably never committed themselves to anything like it before in their lives.

P: Do the young apprentices from this physical community, this neighborhood, take an interest in the spiritual community here at the cathedral?

AB: Some do, and obviously some don't. I think to an extent, even with the ones who say they don't, there's something going on within, which maybe they're not readily going to admit. But when a person insists that this is just a job, I don't really accept that. There has to be something beyond that. I don't think you can give as much concentration and patience as it requires otherwise; the reward monetarily is certainly not there. Then there has to be something else. And that has to come from beyond.

P: How do you recognize a potential apprentice?

AB: You don't. I think basically what you do is you take them on a trial basis for a beginning, which has to be at least three months.

P: Do they come to you?

AB: Yes, and you just look for the patience and the concentration and a willingness to learn. You can't ask for more. No skill at all. You do not expect any skills, nor should you.

P: And what is the sign of success in this apprenticeship?

AB: I think the greatest thing here will be not when a tower is finished, or any part of the cathedral is finished, but when the kids of the next generation walk through that door and say I want to continue what my father did or my mother did. That's when we will have achieved something.

P: You have a son who's just started as an apprentice mason, don't you?

AB: Yes. He's done just over a year in his apprenticeship, and it's changed his life. He seems to expand himself in the stone. He's now the fourth generation mason in our family. But what I'm really looking for is to see the second generation from the young Americans from this neighborhood walk through that door. For them to get started. But maybe I've gone from A to B at least, because the guys that I trained and helped train ten years ago are now starting to help train my son.

P: Where did his wish come from? Was it your wish or his? Because you are third generation, you probably hoped that he would continue, but it really has to be his own wish, doesn't it?

AB: It's a very interesting question. I don't know if I really can answer it. Because I never really expected it to happen. I don't know whether it's because I wanted it so much, and so I put it in the back of my mind and said, well, it's never going to happen. But am I proud about it? Yes, I am. And I want him to be better than what I was. Did he really want it? I don't know. I can't answer that question. He's only seventeen. I don't think he can answer it.

P: You can teach someone technique, but it has to be more than skill, more than technique, doesn't it? And can you teach that?

AB: It has to come from the heart, and you can't teach that.

P: I've been in many, many churches in my life, and a number of cathedrals, and very seldom do I ever really feel anything when I walk in. But you can feel it here, and you can sometimes feel it even in a tiny little country church, way out in the middle of nowhere. In very special cases. You walk in, and you don't know why. But it seems to have something to do with the way that building was *made*, and the way people *are* when they worship there. Something is left behind by all that. As if the buildings were a vessel or container of something very powerful.

AB: I have that very special feeling in the church where my grandfather and grandmother are buried, and also worshiped, an old Norman church called St. Mary Magdalene in Chewton Mendip in Somerset, England. I can't explain it. But I can feel a presence, and I'm overwhelmed by it. It's something I just can't explain. Sometimes it's stronger than others, particularly if there's a wedding or an event that's happening, especially pertaining to me. But I can't walk in that church without feeling that there is something very special there, meaningful to *me*.

I know what you're talking about: it must have something to do with how the church was made. But I find it very difficult to talk about that or to help an apprentice conceive of it or understand it. It's very individual, very special unto oneself.

But as we evolve here in the craft, more and more people will start to experience and understand what goes on and what goes beyond the craft. That has to be experienced, felt. It can't be taught or described. ●

Birth of a Sculpture

Henri Tracol

Henri Tracol, journalist, photographer, and sculptor, formerly with the Musée de l'Homme in Paris, has been twice interviewed in PARABOLA. *His article "Why Sleepest Thou, O Lord?" gave its title to an anthology of his essays and interviews published in France in 1983 under the title* Pourquoi dors-tu Seigneur? *The following is a transcript, translated from that book, of his answers to the questions of a journalist, broadcast December 7, 1981 by the France-Culture network, on Pierre Descargues' program "Le Monde au singulier."*

HENRI TRACOL: In order to avoid any misunderstanding, let me say that I am not a professional sculptor: I haven't studied at any school of fine arts or even taken part in workshops; at most, I've received some enlightening advice from sculptor friends who have encouraged me to follow what I might well describe as a kind of calling.

Certainly I have the greatest respect for the *craft,* for its rules, its standards, its requirements—its tools, equipment, etc.—and of course above all for the material, for the substance itself, which is in no way being violated, destroyed or reduced to nothing, but on the contrary, is being called to life, its own life.

What does this still, silent block of stone wish to say? It is as if it were waiting for me to find its true form through myself. And when I am asked this question, another question is bound to echo in me: I ask myself what "I" wish to say, what is the meaning of my presence on earth, what meaning can I discover in this unknown presence, in this unknown that I am.

QUESTION: Then we could say that art is self-knowledge—and also that self-knowledge is an art?

HT: Without a doubt. It is an art which has its own laws, laws which cannot be broken. But I am systematically anti-systematic: I am always careful not to fall into the trap of "thinking I understand" just because I have had a glimmering of certain ideas which are quite plausible but which have not been part of my experience.

To be precise, I believe the most important thing here is to *enter* into the experience, to feel that one is the material on which all sorts of relatively independent forces are acting. What allows me to be in a certain way the sculptor of myself, or at least to cooperate with the forces that shape me? If I don't do that, I am letting these forces operate and make whatever they wish of me. Nevertheless something in me is called on: as a human being, I am invited to take part in my own formation. And perhaps it is that which more and more strengthens my interest in self-knowledge through the experience of art—not an intellectual interest but one that is much more profound and comes from a deeper source.

Q: How would you relate this very self-knowledge, this immersion in the experience that you just spoke of, with what is called the theory of knowledge? How is the way to be found?

HT: How is the way to be found? Perhaps a whole lifetime would not be enough for that. But it is possible to search, to search honestly. We are led astray by images of what we thought we understood from reading books and listening to "experts." Whether or not I am working on a sculpture, I need to feel that I am directly concerned, that again and again I give myself to the task as directly as possible. I try to make myself available in such a way that I can be conscious of the forces that pass through me, in order to understand better their direction and orientation, and adapt myself better to them; to try to become a good instrument—and a conscious one.

HERE the mystery reappears: how can I be a conscious instrument of the forces which pass through me and define me? How can I be a workman in this work which is in process, at the same time *knowing* it, with the beginning of autonomy, with something which truly obliges me to try to see what corresponds best with what my real self calls me to be?

There is a sentence from Elie Faure which has haunted me since my adolescence, that echoes what I have just tried to say: "The only man who adds to the spiritual wealth of humanity is the one who has the force to become what he is." ●

Les Compagnons du Devoir

IT IS KNOWN THAT the builders of churches were united in fraternities, brotherhoods or guilds. Of brotherhoods there were three—*The Children of Father Soubise, The Children of Master Jacques* and *The Children of Solomon.* They have not totally disappeared; they left heirs who are known now as *Les Compagnons des Devoirs du Tour de France,* a title given them in the nineteenth century. Some of them seem to have observed a tradition of initiation, some not; but all observe a tradition of their calling, a moral tradition of chivalry within their craft and submission to work that *must* be done.

A tale is current regarding them.

Three men were at work in a stone-yard. A passer-by asked them, "What are you doing?"

"I'm earning my bread," said the first.

"I'm following my trade," said the second.

"I'm building a cathedral," said the third. He was a Companion.[1]

—*Louis Charpentier*

At present, the organization is called Les Compagnons du Devoir *and its members engage in other crafts besides masonry, such as shoemaking, metalwork, plumbing, carpentry, and weaving. Jean Bernard, a leader of the present-day Compagnons, writes:*

AMONG THE MANY changes of our time, one which strikes me is in the meaning accepted by our contemporaries of the terms "intellectual" and "manual" as applied to man and his work; in our society they tend to appear under a guise that is as definitive as it is misleading and crude. What is put again in question is that part of man's nature by which he has been known for thousands of years as *homo faber,* "the maker," the ingenious worker with his hands, discoverer of the relation with matter, the father of us all—and above all, the father of our Guild. Later he became *sapiens,* the wise one, the one whose way to control the material world was not only by the simple, rational use of his hands but also by the power of his mind.

The builders of churches were united in fraternities, brotherhoods or guilds.

We are the heirs of both these men; the *faber* and the *sapiens* live in each of us, with infinite variations in the proportion of their mixture. It is an aberration to wish to divide or separate them.

Nothing could offer better conditions than the work of the Companions of Duty for an in-depth study of manual work considered as an essential activity, one that is inherent in human nature. We believe that today, at the beginning of the immense upheavals caused by technology, a new generation is now ready in our Guild for this investigation, without a glance behind, with no reactionary attitude. We do not deny progress; we don't put the manual workers in opposition to the intellectual ones, as it is too easy to do, and so false to think. However, by "manual worker" we do not mean the unskilled laborer, but the workman who creates with his hands, and who has to think in order to create something out of matter. The other are sham manual workers, and like sham intellectuals they are legion.

Gandhi said: "Work with the hands is the apprenticeship of honesty. . . . No one is by nature exempt from the necessity to work with his hands." Above all, he found in it a kind of spiritual exercise applicable to the social renewal of India and so of the whole world. It was not a matter of returning to the past, but of the search for human equilibrium, a kind of wisdom which took into account the human hand and its contact with matter through work, as a means that could help the individual to attain a personal peace; this could generate the harmony and redemption necessary for the peace of the universe. And we must put great emphasis on this: there is no true progress except in each one of us, through our personal effort.

There must be no mistake about the collective aspects of the Guild of the Companions of Duty, which are more developed now than they were formerly to respond to the accumulated needs of the Guild as it is today: they exist only to help each one of its members to become himself, and not to swallow him up.

We think that true communication, love perhaps, cannot arise except through an exchange, and that the mind and the hand, united at the source of movement and its search for completion, and reunited at the moment of highest achievement in the great vocations, are complementary in the deep workings of the whole.[2]

—Jean Bernard

The following statements are from the testimonials of two young Compagnon shoemakers, who happen also to be brothers. The first is still in his period of apprenticeship and is currently on the Tour de France, in Strasbourg. His older brother is an established bootmaker in Paris.

WE GO THROUGH this period of apprenticeship in order to acquire in the hands and in the soul something which can never be lost. Above all, the Guild teaches me to become myself and to give form to that which I wish above all else: to live.

—Christophe Corthay

PART OF MY WORK is repair: what a joy it is to bring back to life a pair of shoes which are old companions to someone who has walked hundreds of kilometers in them; to have the knowledge to work with natural, noble, and living materials: leather, skin, and wood.

Having my own business has brought me great joy, both professionally and personally. It is clear to me today that the Tour de France of the Compagnons du Devoir, with all the values and knowledge that it has given me, brought me to where I am today.

—Pierre Corthay

NOTES

1. From Louis Charpentier, *The Mysteries of Chartres Cathedral*, Ronald Fraser and Janette Jackson, translators (London: Research into Lost Knowledge Organisation, 1972).
2. Translated from *Le Compagnonnage* (Paris: Presses Universaires de France). Originally printed in PARABOLA Vol. X, No. 3, Fall 1985.

ARCS

Tools of Transformation

WE HAVE KNOWN an honor of work exactly similar to that which in the Middle Ages ruled hand and heart. The same honor had been preserved intact, underneath. We have known this care carried to perfection, a perfect whole, perfect to the last infinitesimal detail. We have known this devotion to *l'ouvrage bien faite*, to the good job, carried and maintained to its most exacting claims. During all my childhood I saw chairs being caned exactly in the same spirit, with the same hand and heart as those with which this same people fashioned its cathedrals. . . . [This also entailed] a respect for family, a respect for home. And above all, an innate feeling for respect and a respect for respect itself. A respect for the tool and for the hand, that supreme tool.[1]

—*Charles Péguy*

YOU CAN, if you like, call tools machines or machines tools, but you cannot say there is no difference between doing things the way you intend and doing them the way the designer of the machine or tool intends. . . . The test is always the relation between the work done and the man doing it. If the shape and quality of the things produced are matters for which the workman is responsible, that is one thing; if he is not responsible it is another.[2]

—*Eric Gill*

PEOPLE OUGHT NOT to consider so much what they are to do as what they *are*; let them but *be* good and their ways and deeds will shine brightly. If you are just, your actions will be just too. Do not think that saintliness comes from occupation; it depends rather on what one is. The kind of work we do does not make us holy but we may make it holy. However "sacred" a calling may be, as it is a calling, it has no power to sanctify; but rather we are and have the divine being within, we bless each task we do, be it eating, or sleeping, or watching, or any other. Whatever they do, who have not much of (God's) nature, they work in vain.[3]

—*Meister Eckhart*

THE CHIEF characteristic of handcrafts is that they maintain by their very nature a direct link with the human heart, so that the work always partakes of a human quality. Machine-made things are children of the brain; they are not very human.[4]

—Sōetsu Yanagi

The props assist the house
Until the house is built,
And then the props withdraw—
And adequate, erect,
The house supports itself;
Ceasing to recollect
The auger and the carpenter.
Just such a retrospect
Hath the perfected life,
A past of plank and nail,
And slowness,—then the scaffolds drop—
Affirming it a soul.[5]

—Emily Dickinson

IT WILL ASSIST in understanding the spiritual meaning of a craft, if we look at the implements employed. Having regard to the analogy between the craftsman's activity and the universal or angelic functions, it will be understood that the tools employed by the craftsman are images of what may be called the "macrocosmic tools"; and in this connection it may be recalled that in the symbolism of the most diverse mythologies, tools are often identified with divine attributes. This accounts for the fact that the transmission of initiation was closely connected, in craft initiations, with the bestowal on the craftsman of the tools of the craft; it may therefore be said that the tool is more than the artist, in the sense that its symbolism surpasses the individuality as such.[6]

—Titus Burckhardt

IN MANY PARTS of India to this day, the craftsmen worship their tools at the Daśaharā festival on the day of Viśvakarā Pūjā. From the time of the sūtras, both the materials and the tools of a craft are known to be sacred, for they are the seat of particular powers. The tree which is to be felled by the carpenter or sculptor is propitiated with offerings; he lays his hand on it with a mantra, asking pardon of the spirits residing in the tree. The axe which is to fell the tree is anointed with honey and butter so that the tree is not hurt when the transformation through which a shape of nature becomes a work of art is begun by the craftsman.

Before a craftsman takes up his tools for any particular assignment, the axe, the line, the hammer, and all the other instruments are worshiped with incense, flowers, and unhusked rice, for they are that extension of the craftsman's hand through which he reaches beyond the ranges of his limited human person. All the work is done in a secluded place, with self-control and concentration. The bricks being invoked as goddesses, the material itself is deified prior to the consecration of the building.[7]

—Stella Kramrisch

FOR THE Anglo observer of Navajo sandpaintings, it has always been a source of some bewilderment and frustration that the Navajo "destroy" these sandpaintings in less time than they take to create them. To avoid this overt destruction of beauty and to preserve its artistic value, the Anglo observer always wants to take a photograph of the sandpainting, but the Navajo sees no sense and some danger in that. To the Navajo the artistic or aesthetic value of the sandpainting is found in its creation, not in its preservation. Its ritual value is in its symbolic or representational power and in its use as a vehicle or conception. Once it has served that purpose, it no longer has any ritual value.[8]

—Gary Witherspoon

THE MASON coordinates materials that were scattered and makes of them the habitation of God: from an indeterminate chaos, which it was, his soul becomes the temple of the divine presence, the temple of which the Universe is the model.[9]

—Frithjof Schuon

Like the clay in the hand of the potter
Who thickens or thins it at his will,
So are we in Thy hand, gracious God,
Forgive our sin, Thy covenant fulfill.

Like a stone in the hand of the mason
Who preserves or breaks it at his will,
So we are in Thy hand, Lord of life,
Forgive our sin, Thy covenant fulfill.

Like iron in the hand of the craftsman
Who forges or cools it at his will,
We are in Thy hand, our Keeper,
Forgive our sin, Thy covenant fulfill.

Like the wheel in the hand of the seaman
Who directs or holds it at his will
So are we in Thy hand, loving God,
Forgive our sin, Thy covenant fulfill.

Like the glass in the hand of the blower
Who dissolves or shapes it at his will,
So are we in Thy hand, God of grace,
Forgive our sin, Thy covenant fulfill.

Like the cloth in the hand of the tailor
Who smoothens or drapes it at his will,
So are we in Thy hand, righteous God,
Forgive our sin, Thy covenant fulfill.

Like silver in the hand of the smelter
Who refines or blends it at his will,
So are we in Thy hand, our Healer,
Forgive our sin, Thy covenant fulfill.[10]

—Yom Kippur prayer

INSPIRATION IS a moment of contact with another reality, the moment when everything at once falls into its proper place, when as it were, the entire structure appears, and every part is seen to be related to the whole. So we cannot deny it exists, nor can we remain indifferent to the experience of this momentary, magical change in our insight. Having had the taste of this other reality (for surely it is not our everyday fare), we yet wait passively for its unpredictable reappearance. We also know that without it we are cut off from the source of our true nourishment, and everything we make is empty, without life, belongs to no organic whole.[11]

—Ilonka Karasz

NOTES

1. Charles Péguy, *Basic Verities: Prose and Poetry*, translated by Ann and Julian Green (New York: Pantheon, 1943), pp. 81, 89.
2. From *A Holy Tradition of Working: Passages from the Writings of Eric Gill* (West Stockbridge, Mass.: Lindisfarne Press, 1983), pp. 108-109.
3. From *Meister Eckhardt: A Modern Translation* by Raymond Bernard Blakney (New York: Harper & Brothers, 1941), p. 6.
4. From *The Unknown Craftsman: A Japanese Insight into Beauty* by Sōetsu Yanagi, adapted by Bernard Leach (Tokyo and New York: Kodansha International Ltd., 1972) p. 107.
5. Emily Dickinson, *The Complete Poems of Emily Dickinson* (Boston: Little, Brown and Company, 1927), p. 265.
6. From "Principles and Methods of Traditional Art" by Titus Burckhardt, in *Art and Thought*, edited by K. Bharatha Iyer (London: Luzac & Company Ltd., 1947), p. 18.
7. From *Traditional India: Structure and Change*, ed. Milton Singer (Philadelphia: American Folklore Society, 1959).
8. From *Language and Art in the Navajo Universe* (Ann Arbor: University of Michigan Press, 1977).
9. From *Spiritual Perspectives and Human Facts*, translated by Macleod Matheson (London: Faber and Faber Limited, 1954.) p. 83.
10. Authorship unknown, translated by Ben Zion Bosker, *The High Holyday Prayer Book: Rosh Hashanah and Yom Kippur* (New York: Hebrew Publishing Co., 1959), p. 285.
11. From *Design Forecast* Vol. I (New York: Aluminum Company of America, 1959), p. 12.

Shaping Space

Harry Remde

SOMETHING IN ME knows a space, but something has forgotten. Perhaps these tools will show me. They sit on benches, shelves, and stands with a patience far beyond my own. They have never failed to help me.

I have been asked about working with hand tools and working with machines. The differences are vital. With the hand tool I am in contact with the wood; I can know it as much as I wish—almost fiber by fiber. The tool pauses and proceeds. I finely tune the mallet's strike to work it into corners. I know the chisel's handle as my body knows itself. When I touch the wood with feeling, I can know a better state.

The body of the craftsman is alert to what he needs. He pivots in the moment—is exercised by change. Not so, the machine, which has a narrower gaze. Its changes are geometric. There is not the starting and stopping that seems a sort of breathing. The craftsman's way is like the bending of trees. The machine's way is like the straightness of poles.

The machine is a powerful muscle; within its limit it works superbly. What do I gain by asking for its service?

My shop has four large saws, driven by powerful motors. Their blades are rimmed like chisel's teeth—small, but harder than knives. They bite the wood in increments—thousands of times each second. I watch the narrow path (or "kerf") they leave behind their cutting.

The purity of repetition—how the saw cuts; how the craftsman builds—shows kinship with a calculus whose increments add up as the pile of sawdust grows. Each bite of the saw—each little effort—helps get the job done.

Am I a machine? It is a lingering thought. A machine running a machine? But a motor runs this saw! If I push the wood too fast, the motor slows a bit. There is a limit to its power. It "knows" its inner structure.

Is it not the same within myself? Something compels; something resists. In the moment's chasm between the two, I find my way and take it.

The craftsman knows these two machines: the one outside and the one inside him. When he accepts what they can offer, a bonding grows between them.

WOODWORKING IS a cutting. It is done in every style. The cutters have many forms and many dimensions. Some cut with their sides (the shapers). Some have wide teeth (the jointer-planers). Some cut with their tips (the drills). The commonest ones are circular (the table

As there is strength in art,
so is there art in strength.

---

and radial saws), and linear (the band and scroll saws). They all have hand-held equivalents.

I like these large machines that dwell in iron castings. They come alive for me. I know what they can do. I talk to them inside. Perhaps I'm speaking to myself, but it seems to make connection. Particularly with the bandsaw, which is the most alive of all.

"Nothing cuts like a bandsaw," said my friend at a machinery company when I asked about getting this machine for my shop. The saw I bought was a beauty—old but not much used—built by a company long defunct (perhaps because it built too well!). I got it cheap. Four of us lifted it into the station wagon.

Unlike the thin steel casings of many modern tools, this saw had cast iron, inviolable to bending. I felt a joy in opening and shutting the heavy doors that enclosed the driving wheels. The only signs of age were the rubber "tires" on the wheels; they were pitted and had to be scraped off. It took the puffing strength of three men to stretch the new tires into place. I built a stand of redwood, with the motor swung below to keep a tension on the driving belt.

A sculptor friend stopped in to see. "Cosmic!" was what she said.

I do admit—for all its size and weight, it is a pretty thing!

Unlike other powered saws, the teeth of a bandsaw blade are pulled—not pushed—through the wood. The blade is thin, weighing only ounces. The duty of the heavy frame is to hold it tight and steady. Up to a point, I bless every pound of iron and steel there is in a machine.

As there is strength in art, so is there art in strength. I was brought to this one day when a designer with whom I worked saw a stand I built for all my powered sharpeners. He looked at it awhile and then opined it was a real work of art. Its simple beams, in minimal disguise, disclosed the strengths and directions of all the forces on it.

There are three benches in the shop—a long one against a wall, and two eight-footers down the center. These two are "walk-arounds"; I can see from every direction. The tops overhang the sides—vital in clamping cabinets. They are tempered hardboard on a plywood underlay. Their surfaces, much stained, are like maps of where I've been. On each bench, I set the vises in pairs to handle long boards.

Something must be offered—something given to these machines. They must be cleaned and oiled; abrading surfaces changed. For lack of this, there will be a forfeiture. But something else is needed—a climate in ourselves by which to know the cutting: how hard to press, how fast or slow to move, the very sound of it. Each machine is different, but it cuts in some known way. The separate pieces—when assembled—will be a table, a cabinet, a chair.

There is no "fancy" in the shop, but "fact," delightfully exposed. Heaviness and lightness sit, agreeable—side by side.

There is a knowledge in the shop that counsels the working there. The craftsman places the machines according to their needs. He notes the lengths and widths they cut by the space he leaves around them.

Feeling takes the shape of space—a real geometry. Push space around! Don't give up. You will know it when you find it. It fills our best attention. It is the way we practice for everything we build.

SPACES HAVE voices; everything tells. The benches, themselves, are silent signs. I place them where I want them, then adjust a little bit. In the shop this is equivalent to the way I touch the wood.

I like the sound of shapes (and shapes of sound); a quarter inch can make a difference. My senses all are joined in some brief way. I am a machine myself—open on every side.

What is this opening? It is the craftsman's way. It comes when he's not looking. To his honor he accepts it. It is the genesis of design.

Design is found everywhere and is received from everywhere—but not by thinking about it; I am so bathed in its pure water that I forget to know I see it. It is perpetual in me. Like water, it conforms to all my surfaces. Nothing is lost; nothing left out. I am bound most gently by it.

But I am a creature of appraisal. I think to weigh; I measure flatly. My thought is filled with images. But design is gentle; design is heard. It gathers in abandonment. ●

MICHAEL PROVOST

EPICYCLE

The Hose-Maker / Jewish

Once, in the course of a journey, the Baal Shem stopped in a little town whose name has not come down to us. One morning, before prayer, he smoked his pipe as usual and looked out of the window. He saw a man go by. He carried his prayer shawl and phylacteries in his hand and set his feet as intently and solemnly as though he were going straight to the doors of Heaven. The Baal Shem asked the disciple in whose house he was staying, who the man was. He was told that he was a hose-maker who went to the House of Prayer day after day, both summer and winter, and said his prayer even when the prescribed quorum of ten worshippers was not complete. The Baal Shem wanted to have the man brought to him, but his host said: "That fool would not stop on his way—not if the emperor called him in person."

After prayer, the Baal Shem sent someone to the man with the message that he should bring him four pairs of hose. Soon after, the man stood before him and displayed his wares. They were of good sheep's wool and well-made. "What do you want for a pair?" asked Rabbi Israel.

"One-and-a-half gulden."

"I suppose you will be satisfied with one gulden."

"Then I should have said one gulden," the man replied.

The Baal Shem instantly paid him what he had asked. Then he went on questioning him. "How do you spend your days?"

"I ply my trade," said the man.

"And how do you ply it?"

"I work until I have forty or fifty pairs of hose. Then I put them into a mold with hot water and press them until they are as they should be."

"And how do you sell them?"

"I don't leave my house. The merchants come to me to buy. They also bring me good wool they have bought for me, and I pay them for their pains. This time

BARBARA GARRISON

I left my house only to honor the rabbi."

"And when you get up in the morning, what do you do before you go to pray?"

"I make hose then, too."

"And what psalms do you recite?"

"I say those psalms which I know by heart, while I work," said the man.

When the hose-maker had gone home, the Baal Shem said to the disciples who stood around him: "Today you have seen the cornerstone which will uphold the Temple until the Messiah comes."

CHRIS PETERS

The Basket and World Renewal

Julian Lang

BY TODAY'S standards the task of weaving a basket must seem silly to some, compared to deep space exploration or the transmittal of data concerning the origin of the universe. After all, a basket consists of woven sticks, plaited together into containers. Some of us put our dirty clothes into a basket, but for the most part, basketry has fallen into disuse if not obsolescence. It seems the time has passed when basketry was marveled at for its utility and perfected design. In northwestern California, however, a uniquely-shaped, non-utilitarian basket is still essential to three local Indian tribes for conducting their ceremonies to "fix the world." Without the baskets the Hupa, Karuk, and Yurok would not be able to perform the highly important Jump Dance without solving extremely difficult problems and taking drastic measures.

I am a Karuk Indian and have held these dance baskets in my hands many times. Each possesses its own weight, shape, and danceability. Some of these baskets display the innovative mark of the artist, while others suggest strict adherence to traditional proportion and construction. Whatever the sensibility of the weaver, the baskets are known to the Karuk people as *vikapuhich*; the Yurok call them *e'gor*; the Hupa say *na'wech*. Their curious cylindrical shape suggests the feminine; their decoration, the sublime. These little baskets are found nowhere else in the world. Within our traditional culture and psyche, the baskets are like jewels.

In order for us to fully appreciate the role that baskets play in our ceremonies and life, it is necessary to look to our *pikva*, our stories, and also to the voices of our oldest generations. The stories give us a glimpse of the foundation of our cultural identity. When we saw the high regard in which the white man held the Bible, we translated it into our language as *apxantinihichpikva*, or "white man's myths."

One of many stories about basket weaving takes place during the *pikvahahirak* ("myth-time-and-place"),

Within our traditional culture and psyche, the baskets are like jewels.

CHRIS PETERS

when an Ikxaréeyav family (the Ikxaréeyav are the Spirit-beings of the *pikva* stories) lived in a good way until the father abandoned them in favor of a new wife, and their family life was disrupted. The jilted mother told the children they were going "a different way." They were going to be transformed. The father knew this was about to happen and returned to the house of his first wife, but it had already been abandoned. He caught up with his family on the hillside above the ranch and killed them in a fit of blind rage. Before dying, the wife cursed him, "You will be nothing once Human has arrived! Human will have nothing to do with you! We will be sitting in front of Human (at the annual World Renewal ceremonies). We will be beauty!" The slain family then metamorphosed into the materials used to weave a basket: hazel, willow, bull pine, maidenhair fern, and woodwardia fern. Thus, basketry materials are to us not just natural fibers, but gifts of divine origin.

The three local tribes perform the Jump Dance as part of the ceremony to fix the world. This dance is a ten-day ceremony that is held to rid the earth of sickness and other potential natural catastrophes. It is solemn, ecstatic, and beautiful in its simplicity. The songs are slow and sonorous. Each song begins quietly but is repeated at a higher pitch and intensity as it continues. In steady cadence a line of male dancers stamps the earth to rid it of sickness and all bad thoughts, to set the world back on its axis. Each stamp is followed by the swift lifting heavenward of a smallish, cylindrical basket that we call a *vikapuhich*. The body of the basket is decorated with bold, shiny black designs on a creamy ground. It has been split lengthwise and attached to a hazel stick handle that is wrapped in finely tanned buckskin. A small bunch of yellowhammer feathers is attached at one end.

A popular symbolic interpretation of this basket is that of family, home, and village. The *vikapuhich* contains a prayer for the world to be in balance. The basket is lifted to heaven and then retracted, bringing with it the spirit world's acknowledgment and luck. In unison the line of dancers then stamp out all that is bad. Over and over the basket is raised, then retracted, followed by the stamping out of sickness. Accompanied by songs originally inspired by the wind, the dance soon brings on a collective illumination: the elders cry, the young yearn.

LAST FALL I attended the Yurok Jump Dance at Pekwon, an ancient village about fifteen miles from the mouth of the Klamath River. After ten days, the time of the culmination dance had arrived. I had the distinct honor of choreographing the Pekwon camp's display of wealth, when all the regalia that has been contributed is brought out "to dance," in accordance with Indian law. So, the dance skirts of deerhide were laid out on the earthen floor. Then I brought armload after armload of Jump Dance baskets into the open air ceremonial house. They were stacked into a pile to hip level and four feet long. I carried into the house the fifty necklaces of shell and glass beads which were then laid across the baskets. I brought in the four remaining broad buckskin headbands, each decorated with the brilliant crimson-scarlet of at least forty pileated woodpeckers. Finally, the fifty eagle feather plumes were sent in, making a magnificent sight.

I ran back to the regalia-camp to make sure that nothing had been left behind. As I was returning to the dance, I heard someone running up behind me. I turned and saw a Yurok man named Pordie Blake. He said, "Here. Put this in. I just finished it up this morning," and handed me a small, twelve-inch-long Jump Dance basket. It was pure white except for the dark orange-shafted yellowhammer feathers bunched at its end, and the shiny black design that ran along its side. I immediately perceived it as a newborn. It was light, perfect in proportion, and wonderful to behold. The spectators were already visibly transfixed by the sheer volume of regalia and the frenzy for which the culmination dance is noted. Nevertheless, as I carried the new little basket into the dance house, there was an audible sigh, a look-at-the-beautiful-baby sigh. The world renewal was now complete with the entrance of the basket.

Ada Charles, the white-haired Yurok woman who had woven the little basket cylinder, sat with Pordie, the regalia maker in his mid-forties who had assembled its parts (the hazel stick, yellowhammer feathers, and buckskin) into its finished state. Earlier in the week the Pekwon dancemakers had choreographed a tribute dance to Ada. Each of nine dancers had held a basket she had made. The central dancer had lifted to heaven the first Jump Dance basket she had ever made, back when she was sixteen years old. Included in the line had been a brand new basket, the companion to the little basket I was about to carry into the dance house. The world was being made with the old and the new.

Twenty-two men and four women dance in the culmination dance. Each man raises a basket into the air, and then stamps out all sickness and bad thoughts. In the end the dancers separate into two lines, one side going west and one side going east. They dance and sing pointing the baskets north and south, and then into the sunrise and sunset. They spread their prayers all around this world and the sky-world and bring back the luck. They fix the world for us all.

I am a singer and dancer, and oddly, this was the first dance at which I participated as a spectator. For the first time I saw the weavers and regalia makers "look on" at the dance. Guests to the ceremony are invariably moved by the experience. It is truly a wonderful spectacle, and it is repeated every two years. The basket-makers and owners bring out the baskets, and prepare them, telling their families and friends where each basket came from, who wove it, and how their family came to own it. All along the Klamath River the baskets come out. We believe the baskets are alive and want to dance. That is why they were created, to help us fix the world. ●

EPICYCLE

Marionettes / Hindu

ONE DAY, as they walked in the garden of paradise, Parvati turned to her blue-throated husband Shiva and said, "Let us go down among the people of earth and see how life goes for them." So the two heavenly beings descended to earth in the forms of a young husband and wife. Dressed in white, they appeared in the marketplace of an ancient and high-walled city.

As they walked among the vendors, a small boy ran up to Parvati and placed a crimson flower in her hand. "For the beautiful lady," he said shyly and ran off. Parvati gracefully put the flower in her hair, and the heavenly pair continued on their way.

They soon came upon the part of the market where merchants sold herbs and spices of every kind and color. Coriander and cumin, cardamom and turmeric, were presented in great abundance. Cinnamon, cloves, nutmeg, and ginger were offered to every passer-by. Everywhere the smells hung rich and heavy in the air. As they moved through the market, they came upon displays of finely crafted metalwork and jewelry worked in gold and silver filigree. On every corner could be seen extravagantly colored pottery of every size and shape.

It was not long before they came to a carpenter's shop, where they saw a group of children crowded around the work bench. As they moved closer they saw two beautifully carved dolls. One was costumed as a boy, the other as a girl. Each doll had been carved with finely crafted joints, so that the arms and legs could easily move.

On seeing the dolls, the two gods laughed in delight, and they left the forms of the young couple and entered into the forms of the wooden figures. Each doll rose slowly before the amazed children. Their eyes grew big and round as the little figures stood before them on the carpenter's bench and began to dance. Round and round they moved, to and fro, back and forth the figures danced in an intricate pattern of steps.

After a while Shiva and Parvati grew tired of the dance, and letting the little wooden figures drop lifelessly to the workbench, they returned once more to the shapes of the young couple standing in the street behind the children. Then they turned and continued on their way.

THE CHILDREN, however, were left gazing with disappointment at the little wooden figures lying on the bench. "Make them dance. Make them dance," they begged the carpenter.

The carpenter looked for a moment at the dolls he had made for the children. Then he took a ball of thread and cut the thread into various lengths. He tied each length of thread to a joint on the wooden dolls. When he had done with the dolls, he tied the other ends of each thread to his fingers. Then the carpenter lifted the dolls up by the threads. Slowly and awkwardly he made the dolls dance once again. Round and round, to and fro they danced, and the children once more gazed in delight at the dancing figures.

Shiva and Parvati stopped at the end of the street. They turned and saw what the carpenter had done. Looking at each other, they smiled and vanished.

—Retold by Tom White

TANGENT

Material Worlds

Rob Baker

ATLAS: an opera in three parts. *By Meredith Monk.* Music and choreography by Meredith Monk. Directed by Meredith Monk with Pablo Vela. Art direction by Yoshio Yabara. Lighting by Beverly Emmons. Houston Grand Opera, Houston, Feb. 22-28, 1991; Walker Arts Center, Minneapolis, March 5-6, 1991; Wexner Center for the Arts, Columbus, Ohio, March 9, 1991; American Music Theater Festival, Philadelphia, June 6-9, 1991; Hebbel Theater, Berlin, July 10-14; Odeon Theater, Paris, July 17-20.

Since I work as a mosaicist, building my pieces out of modules of music, movement, character, light, image, text and object, it is difficult to describe "Ghost Stories" in an absolute manner at this point in my process. I am at the stage of gathering my materials, discovering the strands which I will later weave together. What I am working with is three different manifestations of this basic theme. I am allowing the ideas to come for all three, knowing that possibly and probably they will combine in some way—these three islands will connect underwater to form one whole.[1]

When Meredith Monk began planning *ATLAS: an opera in three parts* in 1985, she used the working title of *Ghost Stories* and had three distinctly different plot summaries in mind: a piece based on the life and travels of Alexandra David-Neel, the first Western woman to enter Tibet; a collection of ghost stories, including one from Lafcadio Hearn's *Kwaidan*; and a science-fiction epic of her own design, in a sort of late-Doris-Lessing mode, in which a visitor sent from a more harmonious world visits the Earth at different points in history. With typical spunk, Monk combined all three ideas into one two-and-a-half-hour opera, which now takes David-Neel's life not literally, but as a metaphor for search: the journey of an individual, both alone and with companions, through a succession of geographies, cultures, conditions and confrontations to reach a level of integration and initiation somewhere near the end—or perhaps the beginning—of a life. Like all of Monk's creations, *ATLAS* contains itself simply and unpretentiously, revealing (as Monk's notes hint) "the loss of wonder, mystery and freshness in our contemporary life and the possibility of rediscovering our inherent clarity."[2]

Monk makes containers for sounds and symbols, images and ideas. She is a choreographer, a composer, and a filmmaker, as well as a unique and gifted solo singer and performer. Her works defy categorization: they make real sense only in the context of their own unified multi-media vision and are the result of a constant, careful crafting of material, filtered through a strong conceptual perspective which is not so much iconoclastic or avant-garde as it is evocative of something buried deep in the personal and collective psyche. The very titles of her pieces reflect the personal/universal material she refines as well as the containers she fashions for and out of those elements: *Juice. Vessel. Book of Days. Quarry. Recent Ruins. Education of a Girlchild. The Games.*

Throughout her experiments in dance, theater, and music over the past twenty-five years, Monk has consistently explored the theme of exploration itself, always starting with self-examination. That search has led her to probe both the past, including her own Jewish heritage, and a multi-dimensional present seen through constantly shifting perspectives. Monk's intent seems always to have been not so much to alienate the audience, as in the theatrical credo of Bertolt Brecht, as to surprise or shock them into a new way of seeing.

Her past works all build on this idea of search as both content and style. *Education of a Girlchild* is a reverse-time journey of an elderly woman travelling back toward her own beginning, moving and singing her way through old age, maturity, adolescence, childhood, and infancy. In *The Games* (a collaboration with Ping Chong), a futuristic, post-nuclear-holocaust society tries to make sense of relics left over from a lost age that the audience slowly recognizes as its own present. In the film *Book of Days*, a modern-day excavation team dynamites its way through an ancient,

crumbling wall to discover a palimpsest of a medieval past; a deadpan TV-interviewer's disembodied voice then grills the residents of a long-lost community from the Middle Ages, asking them about their work, their tools, their beliefs and daily life, while an AIDS-like plague starts to sweep through the community.

Occasionally Monk's performances are vast in scope, taking place in spaces as large as the spiralling cavity of the Guggenheim Museum or the dinosaur room of the Smithsonian Institution. At other times, they are private and intimate: chamber pieces in Monk's own living loft, where she once had a sort of Sunday morning coffee hour/salon. But whatever their scale, they exhibit an attention to detail that always gives them a handmade, personal touch: even the playbills usually feature hand-lettered type and a childlike illustration, drawn by Monk herself. Thematically as well, the microcosm and macrocosm are both attended to, ranging from *Small Scroll* to *ATLAS*, the latter of which is both a mountain and a book of maps, both the god who supports the universe on his shoulders and a diagram of that divine plan.

From the beginning, Monk has created consciously and carefully with the material she is most qualified to examine: her own body, her own voice, feelings, and ideas. She has been insistently honest and demanding in this search, and the result is singular, even discomfiting: it doesn't sound or look in the least conventional. At the same time it has remained open, flexible, exploratory—and free of the ego-shackled pretensions that mar the work of so many of her experimental contemporaries.

Musically, Monk consistently reexamines the range and potential of the human voice, over accompaniments involving primarily keyboards (and occasionally strings or reeds) playing simple melodic patterns. Critics (even the more polite ones) usually resort to terms like "keening," "chattering," and "niggling" to describe the specifics of Monk's vocal vocabulary. Tiny gradations of sound, microtonal shifts, combine with strange, otherworldly harmonies. There are seldom lyrics—*ATLAS* has no libretto, per se—but the yips and yelps and squeaks and nonsense syllables take on their own primal significance, more clearly expressing what Monk has referred to as "emotions we have no words for."[3]

MONK IS AN artist who constantly tinkers with her works, making slight adjustments and modifications. She personally dislikes the attitude that anything alive, such as performance, is ever "finished" and bemoans the fact that funding agencies and audiences often force those who create to "constantly come up with 'something new' every year or season."[4] So *ATLAS* will undoubtedly change from venue to venue, performance to performance. But at its première in Houston, it already had the look and sound of a major statement in Monk's growing canon. Whether it qualifies as opera, in Houston or anywhere, is perhaps a moot point. It certainly takes its place in a new late twentieth-century musical-theater genre that directors like Robert Wilson and composers like Philip Glass have helped define.

The scenario opens with a young girl (Dina Emerson) sitting on a bed in her room, then examining a lighted globe and gazing out a window at the stars, including the Big Dipper, a recurring visual motif in the piece. In the next room her mother (Wendy Hill) irons, while her father (Thomas Bogdan) cleans his record collection. The girl dreams of a horse—another recurring motif—and makes little flying and swimming and riding motions with her arms. The silhouette of the horse splits open and out pop the silhouettes of two "guides," one male (Ching Gonzalez), one female (Allison Easter)—anima and animus perhaps. The girl packs her bag, walks to the center of the stage, sets it down. A middle-aged woman (Monk herself) appears from the rear and walks up behind the girl, picks up the suitcase, and takes over the role of the protagonist.

This character then interviews candidates for an expedition, choosing two (Chen Shizheng and Robert Een) and rejecting one (Stephen Kalm), who seems to have an ego problem and sings out of tune. The other three wait impatiently in an airport as various tourists come and go and a janitor pushes a broom back and forth across the stage, staring blankly at the audience.

Various adventures ensue in what seem to be an African or Polynesian village, an Arctic bar (where the music turns country and western with an East European flavor, and everybody dances), a desert, and finally a mountainous region which might be Tibet. Along the line, the egotistical candidate reappears, having learned to carry a tune, and is allowed to join the expedition, as is a West Indian woman (Dana Hanchard) who pops up in the Arctic bar.

The guides reappear periodically, dancing a path for the travellers to follow. Various ghost-visions appear and are responsible for some of the most stunningly visual moments in the work (assisted especially by the eerie colored lighting by Beverly Emmons). At one point one companion is almost frozen by his confrontation with four Ice Demons; the other travellers warm him back to life by bending over his frozen form. At another point, Monk listens too kindly to the sad keening of a Lonely Spirit (counter tenor Randall Wong), only to find herself trapped in a circle afterwards (like the Yezidi child in Peter Brook's film of *Meetings with Remarkable Men*), but again the companions manage, all together, to spring her free.

The group comes upon an Ancient Man (Wilbur Pauley), sitting center stage with an immensely long flowing beard of green vegetation. The searchers step carefully along the separate paths of his beard and eventually are allowed to ask three questions, all of which get mysterious replies. Monk's character stays on alone to talk to the old man.

Violence, dissension, sexual frustrations break out; group members become ill, depressed, angry, mad. Een's character goes completely crazy and has to be left behind as the other four climb up a ladder in the center of the stage at the end of the second act.

Act Three is short, haunting, mysterious. The travellers arrive at a higher world at the other end of the ladder they started up before the curtain fell. There they find their guides and a group of people, an organization or society of some sort. The music becomes chantlike, the movements ceremonial: without either becoming directly imitative of any specific tradition, the overall tone or quality of the scene is definitely Tibetan. The four travellers are given the same black robes that others in the community wear.

Monk moves forward carrying her suitcase and puts it down beside her on the stage. An older woman (Sally Gross) comes up from behind. Monk exits stage right and Gross takes up the suitcase and becomes the character in old age. She walks forward to a table and chair, sits down, and, self-contained at last, pours herself a cup of coffee.

The stage lights come up dimly on the child's bedroom from the first scene, with the searcher's two younger selves now sitting quietly on the bed.

> The process of making a piece is very much like a quest; you start out in the dark; you have a sense of the potential that opens out before you; there is a sense of danger because no one has gone this way before; you follow clues, listen to instincts, look out for what is needed; soon, the way becomes apparent as more and more layers are added in and the piece takes on its own life.[5]

•

NOTES

1. From Meredith Monk's "Statement of Concept" for *Ghost Stories* (later *ATLAS: an opera in three parts*), submitted to the Houston Grand Opera Association and released to the press when *ATLAS* premièred in February, 1991. (Unpublished, p. 1).
2. Monk, "Notes about *ATLAS*," Houston Grand Opera *Stagebill* (Winter, 1991), p. 18.
3. From an interview with Edward Strickland in *Fanfare* (Jan./Feb. 1988).
4. From private conversations with the reviewer.
5. "Statement of Concept," p. 3.

CURRENTS & COMMENTS

PROGRAMS

THE AMERICAN Federation of Arts, New York City (212-988-7700) announces **Gold of Africa: Jewelry and Ornaments from Ghana, Côte D'Ivoire, Mali and Senegal** which will be on view at The Art Institute of Chicago until August 25, and at The Baltimore Museum of Art from September 17 through November 10. The exhibit, including over 200 examples of goldsmith's art and jewelry which range from royal regalia to everyday personal ornaments, will continue to three additional venues in 1992 in Detroit, Louisville, and Memphis. The federation presents a second traveling exhibition, **American Prints in Black-and-White, 1900-1950: Selections from the Reba and Dave Williams Collection** which will be on display until August 24 at the Columbus Museum, Columbus, Georgia, and from September 21 through November 16 at the Newark Museum, Newark, New Jersey, and will continue to six additional venues in 1992. Linked to its roots as an extension of drawing, early twentieth-century printmaking depicted Americans at work in the land and in the cities, in styles that ranged from the realist to the abstract.

The National Museum of the American Indian, New York City (212-283-2420), is displaying **Handwoven Baskets and a Raven's Tail Robe Sampler** in the contemporary exhibit case, through November 10. These examples of traditional weaving methods were made by Teri Rofkar who learned the craft from her grandmother Eliza York, a Tlingit Indian from the Pelican area of Alaska. Also at the museum, programs of story-

telling, music, and dance from the Sac/Fox and Caddo/Potawatomi tribes will be presented at 2 P.M. on October 12 and November 2 by Joe Cross and Donna Couteau. The museum also announces that the ninth annual Native American festival, **Tree Rings: Preserving the Inwood Forest** will be hosted by the Urban Park Rangers on September 14 from 10 A.M. to 6 P.M. (rain date Sept. 15) at Inwood Park on Isham Street and Seaman Avenue.

The Arthur M. Sackler Gallery, Washington, DC (202-357-4880), is presenting **Crushed Lapis and Burnished Gold: The Art of Illumination** through December 8. This exhibit of approximately 30 manuscripts, individual folios, and book covers demonstrates the art of illumination and manuscript embellishment that has been a part of book production in the Muslim world since the ninth century, and includes examples of the illuminator's tools and materials. The gallery also announces **Forty Indian Paintings from the Collection of Howard Hodgkin**, on display from September 15 through January 12, 1992, which will include paintings and drawings from the Rajput, Deccani, and Mogul styles of Indian art.

The Asia Society, New York City (212-288-6400), presents **The Here and the Hereafter: Images of Paradise in Islamic Art** until September 8. This exhibition brings together examples of calligraphy, painting, textiles, ceramics, stone carving, metalwork, and architecture relating to the idea of paradise in Islamic art from the ninth to the nineteenth centuries in a region stretching from North Africa to India. The objects are grouped in four sections: "Paradise and the World," which illustrates the pathway to heaven as revealed in the Qur'an; "Paradise Described," showing the Islamic concept of paradise; "Paradise Symbolized," including the metaphorical references to the afterlife; and "Paradise Attained," showing the religious image of the heavenly garden as it figures in the architecture of the Islamic royal palaces.

The Los Angeles County Museum of Art (213-857-6111) announces **The Arts of the Persian World: The A. Soudavar Collection** from September 5 through November 10, which shows the Persian influence on artistic productions from India to Turkey. The exhibit's paintings, drawings, calligraphies, manuscripts, and metalwork, examples of most of the major schools of Persian art, demonstrate the impact of Islam and the Mongol invasions on Persian culture. A selection of paintings from the Safavid period (1501-1736) highlights the collection.

The IBM Gallery of Science and Art, New York City (212-745-6100), announces **Wisdom and Compassion: The Sacred Art of Tibet** from October 15 through December 22. The 160-piece exhibit of bronzes and thangkas span the period from the ninth to the nineteenth centuries; and monks of the Namgyal Monastery will create a colored sand Kalachakra Mandala as part of the display.

CONFERENCES

THE PACIFICA Graduate Institute, Carpinteria, California (805-969-3626), will present **Robert Bly & Marion Woodman: Facing the Male and the Female Shadow** on October 12 and 13 from 10 A.M. to 5 P.M. The two-day conference will focus on the unknown side as it is experienced by men and women.The subject will be examined through an interweaving of story, poetry, talk, and music.

TAPES, BOOKS

FILMAKERS LIBRARY, New York City (124 E. 40 St.), has just released *The Potters of Buur Heybe, Somalia*. This videotape, available for sale or rent, describes the materials and techniques of Somalian pottery, where the women, as the orginal discoverers of clay, mine the clay in community-held pits, while the men, who first discovered the uses of fire, make the pottery.

The Crossing Press, Freedom, California (800-777-1048), has just published *Hoop Snakes, Hide Behinds, & Side-Hill Winders: Adirondack Tall Tales*, told by Joe Bruchac and illustrated by Tom Trujillo. The stories of Bill Greenfield and Grampa Jesse are included, among others.

FULL CIRCLE

A Readers' Forum

I WAS ABSOLUTELY shocked when I received my *last* issue of PARABOLA—"The Hunter." I say last because I am canceling my subscription.

To quote George Bernard Shaw, "While we ourselves are the living graves of murdered beasts, how can we expect any ideal conditions on this earth?" And then to devote an entire issue to the glorification of killing animals and masking it behind a smoke screen of moral self-justification and sentimental imagery was very disturbing to me.

Every major religion's dictum of "thou shalt not kill" is made a mockery of in this issue. The skillful display of writing by the contributors and their supposed "love of animals" coupled with a *seeming* interest in the planet's precarious position does not hold water. These individuals are justifying their inability to see (or want to see) the root of the problem. If they could only understand that, as an ancient Zen master put it, "Heaven and Earth and I are of the same root," that is, that all life is based on the principle of mutual attraction and rightness common to all nature.

—Jorn J. Curtiss

EDITORS' RESPONSE: And, properly seen (rather than sentimentally philosophized about), these forms of life kill each other and are part of each other's nourishment. Our issue made no attempt to take sides or glorify this objective fact, but merely to present it, in order to better understand the real relationship between Heaven and Earth, rather than prescribing it according to one's own moral indignation.

IN ISSUE XI:3 (Aug 1986), Philip Zaleski reviewed Michael Denton's book *Evolution: A Theory in Crisis*. I found the review so valuable that I purchased the book. Denton writes: "The proposition that the genetic programs of higher organisms . . . were composed by a purely random process is an affront to reason."

For centuries scientists have been attempting to explain the origin and functioning of the universe working by a mixture of mechanical laws and random interactions. They reject the possibility of the existence of a purposeful creator with an intelligence incomparable to ours; a concept with which humanity lived for ten thousand years. But the idea that there is more to reality than what we can directly perceive in space and time is not new. Modern physics describes the directly observable world as having three space dimensions and a fourth dimension: time. Some theories of physics have postulated a fifth dimension not directly observable but having indirect effects. In metaphysics this fifth dimension corresponds to the eternal here-now stretching to infinity at right angles to space and time: the Noumena of Kant. Within this extended framework there is room for the idea of the existence of an intelligent, purposeful creator, which includes a purpose in man's life.

—M. W. Thring
Suffolk, England

AS A CHAMPION of "the feminine" and the importance of embracing it in male and female psychology alike, I would seem to be the first to agree with David Apelbaum's conclusion ("Not at Home: The Search for the Father," XV:3) that it is only through the fruitful union of masculine and feminine energies that

(Continued on page 98)

PARABOLA BACK ISSUES

For fifteen years PARABOLA has gathered distinguished writers and thinkers seeking to reach new understandings of the universal human themes as they are expressed in myth and legend, ancient symbol and sacred art, folklore and ritual. Through PARABOLA back issues, you can now share in this storehouse of knowledge and insight. PARABOLA readers treasure their back issues as a permanent part of their libraries, a source of ideas to re-read and reflect on. Each is a beautifully designed, sturdily bound paperback of 128 pages. Back issues are $8.00 per copy; orders of 12 or more, $7.00 per copy.

Please use the order form bound between these pages.

❑ VOL. I:1 **The Hero** Mircea Eliade, Barbara G. Myerhoff, Barre Toelken, P.L. Travers, Jacob Needleman, Edward Edinger, Minor White; Huston Smith interview.

❑ VOL. I:2 **Magic** Barbara G. Myerhoff, Daniel Noel, Robert Ellwood, Jacob Needleman, Victor Turner, Thomas Moore, Christmas Humphreys; Joseph Campbell interview.

❑ VOL. I:3 **Initiation** Sam Gill, Janwillem van de Wetering, Arthur Amiotte, Evelyn Eaton, Fernando Llosa Porras; Mircea Eliade interview.

❑ VOL. I:4 **Rites of Passage** Frederick Franck, James Wolfe, Ursula K. Le Guin, D.M. Dooling, Robert E. Meagher; William Irwin Thompson interview.

❑ VOL. II:1 **Death** P.L. Travers, Conrad Hyers, Isaac Bashevis Singer, David Steindl-Rast, William Doty, William Burke Jr.; Tibetan Lamas interview.

❑ VOL. II:2 **Creation** Sam Gill, P.L. Travers, David Rosenberg, David Johnson, Jane Yolen, John Fentress Gardner, Daniel Whitman; Zalman Schachter interview.

❑ VOL. II:3 **Cosmology** David Steindl-Rast, Ursula K. Le Guin, Lorel Desjardins, Elaine Jahner, Anne Bevan, Harry Remde; Lloyd Motz interview.

❑ VOL. II:4 **Relationships** Frederick Franck, Robert E. Meagher, Shems Friedlander, Lizelle Reymond, Jean Toomer, Barre Toelken, Jane Yolen; Diane Wolkstein interview.

❑ VOL. III:1 **Sacred Space** A.K. Coomaraswamy, Barbara Stoler Miller, Robert Lawlor, Irving Friedman, Pablo Neruda, Hélène Fleury; P.L. Travers and Michael Dames interview.

❑ VOL. III:2 **Sacrifice and Transformation** Annemarie Schimmel, Joseph Epes Brown, Robert A.F. Thurman, Minor White; Adin Steinsaltz interview.

❑ VOL. III:3 **Inner Alchemy** Mircea Eliade, D.M. Dooling, Harry Remde, Jacob Needleman, Elémire Zolla.

❑ VOL. III:4 **Androgyny** Elaine H. Pagels, Titus Burckhardt, Keith Critchlow, P.L. Travers, Barbara G. Myerhoff; Lobsang Lhalungpa interview.

❑ VOL. IV:1 **The Trickster** Emory Sekaquaptewa, Michel Waldberg, Lynda Sexson, Barbara Tedlock, P.L. Travers, David Leeming; Joseh Epes Brown interview.

❑ VOL. IV:2 **Sacred Dance** Elaine H. Pagels, Rosemary Jeanes, David P. McAllester, Fritjof Capra, Annemarie Schimmel; Peter Brook interview.

❑ VOL. IV:3 **The Child** Don Talayesva, Richard Lewis, Frederick Franck, Lynda Sexson, Lobsang Lhalungpa, art and stories by children.

❑ VOL. IV:4 **Storytelling and Education** Maria José Hobday, Thomas Buckley, James Hillman, education symposium.

❑ VOL. V:1 **The Old Ones** Keith Critchlow, Agnes Vanderburg, Lobsang Lhalungpa, Robert Bly, Gary Snyder; Deshung Rinpoche and Joseph Campbell interviews.

❑ VOL. V:2 **Music Sound Silence** Herbert Whone, Tomas Tranströmer, David A. Lavery, Tom Moore, David P. McAllester, Howard Schwartz, Robert Lawlor; Steve Reich interview.

❑ VOL. V:3 **Obstacles** Al Young, Abraham Menashe, David Steindl-Rast, Jonathan Omer-Man; Mohawk Chiefs and the Dalai Lama interviews; photo essay.

❑ VOL. V:4 **Woman** P.L. Travers, Helen M. Luke, Seonaid Robertson, Ursula K. Le Guin, Barbara Rohde, Joseph Campbell; Judy Swamp interview.

❑ VOL. VI:1 **Earth and Spirit** Peter Matthiessen, Peter Nabokov, Robert Bly, Paul Caponigro, P.L. Travers, John Kastan, D.M. Dooling; Firoze M. Kotwal interview.

❑ VOL. VI:2 **The Dream of Progress** Kathleen Raine, David Malouf, Dino Buzzati, Seyyed Hossein Nasr; Chinua Achebe and Jacob Needleman interviews.

❑ VOL. VI:3 **Mask and Metaphor** Terry Tafoya, Ray Zone, Demorest Davenport, Adin Steinsaltz, Henrich von Kleist; Peter Brook interview.

❑ VOL. VI:4 **Demons** J. Stephen Lansing, Maria Dermoût, Chinua Achebe, Susan Stern, Edwin Bernbaum, Dino Buzzati; Isaac Bashevis Singer interview.

❑ VOL. VII:1 **Sleep** Henri Tracol, Mircea Eliade, A.K. Ramanujan, Jonathan Omer-Man, P.L. Travers; Dr. Yeshi Dhonden and Joseph Campbell interviews.

❑ VOL. VII:2 **Dreams and Seeing** Ursula K. Le Guin, Arthur Amiotte, Wendy Doniger O'Flaherty, Elémire Zolla; conversation between Laurens van der Post and P.L. Travers.

❑ VOL. VII:3 **Ceremonies** Joseph Epes Brown, Robertson Davies, Doris Lessing, Francelia Butler, Frederick Franck, Barbara Nimri Aziz, P.L. Travers, David Abram, Joseph Bruchac, David Steindl-Rast.

❑ VOL. VII:4 **Holy War** Jonathan Cott, René Daumal, Seyyed Hossein Nasr, Adin Steinsaltz; David Steindl-Rast interview.

❑ VOL. VIII:1 **Guilt** Vincent Rossi, P.L. Travers, Adin Steinsaltz, John Updike, Robert Granat, Helen M. Luke, Thomas Dooling; Michel de Salzmann interview.

❑ VOL. VIII:2 **Animals** Joseph Epes Brown, Barry Lopez, Dino Buzzati, Paul Shepard, Philip Kapleau, Robert Bly, Ursula K. Le Guin; James Hillman interview.

❑ VOL. VIII:3 **Words of Power** William Chittick, L. Charbonneau-Lassay, P.L. Travers, Richard Lewis; Kathleen Raine interview.

❑ VOL. VIII:4 **Sun and Moon** Martha Heyneman, Martin Lev, Carol Ring, Jonathan Omer-Man, Paul Jordan-Smith; Seyyed Hossein Nasr interview.

❑ VOL. IX:1 **Hierarchy** Henri Tracol, Janwillem van de Wetering, Roger Lipsey, Martin Lings; Adin Steinsaltz interview.

❑ VOL. IX:2 **Theft** Joseph Bruchac, Robert Venables, John Stratton Hawley, Robert A.F. Thurman, Jonathan Omer-Man; David Maybury-Lewis interview.

❑ VOL. IX:3 **Pilgrimage** Arthur Amiotte, Padma Perera, Gai Eaton, Richard R. Niebuhr, Paul Brunton, Thomas Buckley; Tara Tulku interview.

❑ VOL. IX:4 **Food** Martha Heyneman, Padma Perera, Basarab Nicolescu, Ursula K. Le Guin, Christopher Bamford, Lobsang Lhalungpa, Donald Harper; Henri Tracol interview.

❑ VOL. X:1 **Wholeness** Interviews with H.H. the Dalai Lama, Helen M. Luke, Seyyed Hossein Nasr, Geoffrey Chew and Jacob Needleman, Pauline de Dampierre, Kallistos Ware, Kobori Nanrei Roshi, Adin Steinsaltz; special expanded Tenth Anniversary Issue.

❑ VOL. X:2 **Exile** Vine Deloria, Jr., Janwillem van de Wetering, D.M. Dooling, Philip Zaleski, Robert A.F. Thurman, Richard R. Niebuhr, P.L. Travers; Elie Wiesel interview.

❑ VOL. X:3 **The Body** Robert Aitken, Christopher Bamford, Roger Lipsey, Martha Heyneman, Gai Eaton, P.L. Travers, Jean Bernard; essay by and interview with Henri Tracol.

❑ VOL. X:4 **The Seven Deadly Sins** Janwillem van de Wetering, Helen M. Luke, John Loudon, D.M. Dooling, P.L. Travers; Pauline de Dampierre interview.

❑ VOL. XI:1 **The Witness** Richard R. Niebuhr, P.L. Travers, Victor Danner, Julio Cortázar, Thomas A. Dooling; Bede Griffiths interview.

❑ VOL. XI:2 **Mirrors** Jonathan Omer-Man, Jacques Lusseyran, P.L. Travers, D.M. Dooling, Frederick Franck, Peter Brook, Claire R. Farrer, Bernard Second; Helen M. Luke interview.

❑ VOL. XI:3 **Sadness** David Dean Shulman, Peggy V. Beck, Peter Lamborn Wilson, Harry Remde; Tara Tulku interview.

❑ VOL. XI:4 **Memory and Forgetting** Alan McGlashan, Anne Twitty, P.L. Travers, Martha Heyneman, Padma Perera, Daniel Schillaci; Keiji Nishitani interview.

❑ VOL. XII:1 **The Knight and The Hermit** Eknath Easwaran, P.L. Travers, Lewis P. Johnson, Thomas Merton, Paul Jordan-Smith, Sybil Thornton, Barbara Stoler Miller, Dag Hammarskjöld, Nobuyoshi Higashi, Elie Wiesel.

❑ VOL. XII:2 **Addiction** Heinrich Zimmer, Richard S. Sandor, A.R. Orage, Robert Aitken, P.L. Travers, Victor Danner; Marion Woodman and Pauline de Dampierre interviews.

❑ VOL. XII:3 **Forgiveness** D.M. Dooling, Alan McGlashan, P.L. Travers, Ann Belford Ulanov, Roger Lipsey, Paul J. Tillich, James Baldwin, Colin Berg; Thomas Hopko interview.

❑ VOL. XII:4 **The Sense of Humor** Helen M. Luke, P.L. Travers, Joseph Bruchac, Henry Corbin, Richard Lewis, Conrad Hyers, Lee Siegel; a conversation between Speed Vogel and Moshe Waldoks.

❑ VOL. XIII:1 **The Creative Response** William Anderson, Anne Twitty, Rachel Fletcher, Roger Lipsey, William K. Mahony, P.L. Travers, Janet Heyneman; Seyyed Hossein Nasr and Paul Reynard interviews.

❑ VOL. XIII:2 **Repetition and Renewal** Mircea Eliade, Marguerite Yourcenar, Harry Remde, Bill Moyers and Joseph Campbell, P.L. Travers, Ravi Ravindra, P.D. Ouspensky, Gertrude Stein, Thomas Buckley, Linda Hogan, Paul Jordan-Smith; Steve Reich, Lincoln Kirstein and Peter Brook interviews; photo essay.

❑ VOL. XIII:3 **Questions** Eknath Easwaran, Richard Lewis, P.L. Travers, Frederick Franck, John Navone, P.D. Ouspensky, Linda Hogan, Thomas A. Dooling, Martin Buber, Brian Swann, James Karman; a conversation between William Segal and D.M. Dooling.

❑ VOL. XIII:4 **The Mountain** René Daumal, Edwin Bernbaum, P.L. Travers, Paul Jordan-Smith, Richard Temple, Trebbe Johnson, Lama Anagarika Govinda, Helen M. Luke, Rob Baker, Marco Pallis; Thubten Jigme Norbu and Jack Daumal interviews.

❑ VOL. XIV:1 **Disciples and Discipline** Karlfried Graf Dürckheim, Janet Heyneman, Dona S. Gower, Roger Lipsey, Louis Charbonneau-Lassay, Philip Zaleski, Laurence Rosenthal, P.D. Ouspensky; Dennis Thompson interview.

(Continued on page 98)

(Continued from page 97)

(Continued from page 95)

the incomplete can be made whole. However, I believe that he has misread and misrepresented Robert Bly's position—a position that is perhaps clarified by Bly's newly published *Iron John*, which appeared subsequently to the videotape on which Appelbaum bases his critique.

Appelbaum says that Bly has overlooked the feminine side of man's nature. I think he has missed Bly's point. Bly has not overlooked the feminine—in himself or in his work. Rather I believe that he would argue that a man cannot connect with and integrate the feminine side of his nature until he has connected fully with his own essential masculinity. It is this essential masculinity that contemporary men are denied through, Bly would claim, direct contact with their fathers. Appelbaum aptly points out that "The vibrant male hero requires help from the feminine *to return to* [emphasis mine] his integrated human nature." I believe that Bly would say he is discussing an apprehension of a man's own nature rather than a return. He is not talking about "newly transformed life," he is talking about establishing one's life in a manly way.

—*Emily Hancock*
Berkeley, California

YOUR ISSUE on "Hospitality" (XV:4) sparked a great deal of excitement among the board and staff of the non-profit cafe I'm involved with, Sisters of the Road Café. We operate on a philosophy of non-violence, gentle personalism and hospitality, serving homeless and very low-income people. Our meals go for $1.25, or a $1.00 food stamp, or you can barter labor (dish washing, table wiping, sweeping, etc.) for credit on meals. We recognize child care as useful, needed labor and therefore feed

THE BESTIARY OF CHRIST

by Louis Charbonneau-Lassay Translated by D.M. Dooling

A NEW TRANSLATION—THE FIRST EVER IN ENGLISH—OF THE STANDARD WORK OF ANIMAL SYMBOLISM IN CHRISTIAN AND OTHER RELIGIOUS TRADITIONS.

"Accompanied by over 400 of the author's original woodcuts, this is a treasury of the wisdom of symbols, a hidden classic of spiritual literature revealed." —Kirkus Reviews

Hardcover; 496 pages; 400 illustrations; $29.95

DARK WOOD to WHITE ROSE

Journey and Transformation in Dante's Divine Comedy

by Helen M. Luke

In this provocative study, Helen Luke takes the reader on an intense spiritual and symbolic journey of exploration into each of Dante's poetic images. Richly illustrated with reproductions in black and white of medieval manuscript paintings inspired by Dante's masterpiece.

"A proud book with sensitive prose . . . The mystical journey toward wholeness as viewed from a Jungian perspective."
— The Book Reader

Hardcover; 224 pages; 44 illustrations; $19.95

LEANING ON THE MOMENT

Interviews from *PARABOLA* Magazine

Interviews with Joseph Campbell, H.H. the Dalai Lama, Peter Brook, Helen M. Luke, P.L. Travers, Sir Laurens van der Post, Mircea Eliade, Isaac Bashevis Singer, Brother David Steindl-Rast, and seven other luminaries.

"These interviews, so skillfully done, give readers direct access to some remarkable persons . . . lively and intriguing . . . "
—Richard Niebuhr
Hollis Professor of Divinity, Harvard University

Hardcover; 272 pages; 26 photographs; $13.95

THE GARDEN BEHIND THE MOON

A Real Story of the Moon Angel

Written and Illustrated by Howard Pyle

"Best Children's Storybook, 1989"
— Publishers Marketing Assoc.

The long-out-of print children's fantasy tale of a boy drawn by the mysterious Moon Angel into following the moon path to its source. Meant to be read aloud, with over 30 original illustrations and woodcuts.

"Absolutely charming! Like all great mythic stories it delves into all the deepest and darkest questions which the human spirit has asked throughout the ages ."
— Madeleine L'Engle

Hardcover; 192 pp.; over 30 illustrations; $14.95.

AND THERE WAS LIGHT

The Autobiography of Jacques Lusseyran

This previously out-of-print classic is a gripping, heroic story by a man who transcended both blindness and imprisonment in a Nazi concentration camp to develop a unique understanding and love of life. It is a story of blindness and seeing, and how they exist together to create an inner light.

"This is a magical book, the kind that becomes a classic, passed along between friends." — The Baltimore Sun

Paperback; 320 pages; $10.95

OLD AGE

by Helen M. Luke

In this collection of essays, Helen Luke, Jungian counselor and Director of the Apple Farm Community, gives us her challenging thoughts on the transformative mysteries of old age and suffering. "Growing old" is explored as a journey of renewal and new challenges as the Self moves toward completion and wholeness.

"I know of no woman of our time who has made a richer and more significant contribution, in a truly contemporary way, to man's understanding of himself. Her essays on old age are among the finest she has ever done."
— Sir Laurens van der Post

Hardcover; 128 pages; $12.95

A WAY OF WORKING

The Spiritual Dimension of Craft

Edited by D.M. Dooling

In this enriching collection of eleven interrelated essays by a group of authors writing not primarily as individuals but as members of a community, the ancient relationship of art, order, and craft is explored. Craft is considered as a "sort of ark" for the transmission of real knowledge about being, and about our deep creative aspirations.

"This book is not only for any serious craftsman but for everyone who wants to make sense of his one and only life."
— Louise March, Founder and Director, Rochester Folk Art Guild

Paperback; 142 pages; $8.95

All Parabola Books have sewn bindings and are printed on acid-free paper.

Please use the order form bound between pages 96 and 97.

parents with children. We also serve people who have challenges which prevent them from working. We serve about two hundred meals per day. Only about twenty per cent of our budget is supported by food sales; the rest is contributions from individuals (thirty to forty per cent), and major gifts and grants. My specialty on the board is asking people, usually large groups of people, for money.

My only request to you about PARABOLA is that you do more on the feminine and the position of women in spiritual matters and religion. You do a good job of featuring the female exponents of the older traditions and so forth, but you must admit these traditions have done poorly by women and the feminine.

There is a lot out there if you want to go after it. I read recently (in some general interest magazine) that the Tibetan Buddhists have named a tulku in Maryland who could best be described as a chubby suburban matron. What does she have to say? I'd love to know!

What about all the wonderful women ministers (and ministerial couples) in the African-American churches (COGIC, etc.)? What a gold mine of myth and tradition! Talk about love triumphing over hate, faith over cynicism, and hope over despair—in the face of the most persistent, vicious provocation and discouragement. I wonder what they'd say about the feminine incarnation of the divine, women as spiritual teachers, etc.?

Anyway, thank you again for making PARABOLA. I'm very glad you are there.

—Katie Butel
Portland, Oregon

I USED TO subscribe to your publication for a number of years. However, aside from one issue on "Woman" (V:4), you have virtually ignored the powerful mythic themes of goddesses, heroines, witches, and wisewomen. You have failed to touch the heart of any of the magic of the old pre-patriarchal religious motifs. Your broadside currently indicates that you do not plan to change this policy, so I do not wish to renew my subscription and be disappointed again.

If you ever do decide to address any of these mythic themes with issues devoted to female divinity and power, I would be willing to consider resubscribing. I know that I am not the only frustrated feminist theologian that has chosen to spend her money elsewhere because of your lack of female focus. Wishing for change . . .

—Morning Glory Zell
Ukiah, California

I WOULD HAVE considered a subscription, or at least ordering some back issues, until I saw a back issue on "Woman." Up until then, I was considering how many of the topics were of interest to me, such as "Rites of Passage" (I:4) or "Sacred Space" (III:1). But then, when I saw "Woman" as a topic, an *object* to discuss, I realized that I, as a woman, was not thought of by your magazine as a subscriber or a consumer, but as an object to study, not a point of reference. I am, by your objectification, "other" than reader, especially as you choose not to study "Man" as a topic. I am insulted and unwilling to spend money to support you.

—Susan L. Kirk
Sacramento, California

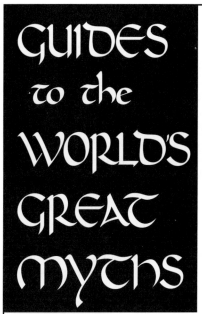

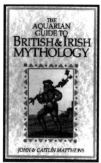

BOOK REVIEWS

Iron John: A Book About Men
By Robert Bly. Reading, Mass.: Addison-Wesley, 1990. Pp. *xi* + 268. $18.95, cloth.

THIS BOOK by the well-known poet Robert Bly is built on an ancient folk tale by the same name ("Iron Hans" in most translations) in the collection by the Brothers Grimm. The original story tells of a wild man (the catalyst of the tale's many twists and turns) who dwells at the bottom of an enchanted well; this wild man helps a young man to become a great warrior and nobleman, while the young man in turn releases Iron John from his ancient curse, allowing the hairy protohuman to regain his original state as a king wealthy beyond all measure.

As suggested by the subtitle, Bly's retelling and analysis of the Grimm tale is "a book about men," and as such it has been widely discussed as the vanguard of the new "men's liberation" movement (it's worth noting that *Iron John* was for much of this past year the best-selling book in the United States, testament to the intense wish of many men to escape what they perceive as suffocating, socially-imposed "male" modes of behavior). However, the temptation to categorize *Iron John* could lead to misconceptions about the book's content and about Bly's intentions. Bly's "liberation" is really better understood as psychological transformation. Men exist in an arrested state of development, he proposes, and the tragedy is that these "men" are unaware that in fact they are not men, but boys. As Bly says, "Our society produces a plentiful supply of boys, but seems to produce fewer and fewer men." And of course a society dominated by boys will have more than its share of problems.

Bly contends that our culture's loss of the initiatory process and of the role of the mentor or guide in that process are the prevailing reasons for men's stunted growth. According to Bly, the character of Iron John—whom he likes to call "the wild man"—symbolizes the role of the mentor. Initiation for Bly can begin only when one comes into contact with the wild man. The wild man apparently plays two roles: first, he is the outer mentor who can guide youth to "manhood," and second, he is an aspect of our inner life (along with other principal roles in the story) that must be (re-)discovered: "The Wild Man lives in complicated interchanges with other interior beings. A whole community of beings is what is called a grown man."

Bly's emphasis on "wholeness" and "transformation" sets him apart from many of the voices that are calling us to an easy "liberation." But problems remain. For "men" to become men signals the accomplishment of the initiatory process outlined in *Iron John*, a goal that is undeniably noble. But the attainment of wholeness as Bly understands it, of becoming a man, might also signal the possible beginning of another initiatory process, that which Carl Jung termed a work towards "perfection."

One wonders, too, whether certain details of the "initiatory process" haven't been diminished in *Iron John* and whether necessary distinctions haven't been glossed over. There is a tendency in books of this sort to pull together admittedly rich and provocative material from various traditions, epochs, and cultures, and to highlight similarities without regard for differences. The treatment in *Iron John* of

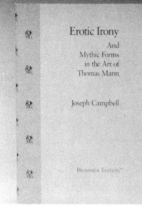

the Sumerian epic of *Gilgamesh* is a case in point: Bly suggests that Enkidu, who is indeed covered with hair and lives in the wilderness, is an ancient parallel to the "wild man" of the Iron John tale. But there are so many differences that questions immediately arise: If Enkidu is the "wild man" in the sense that Bly uses the term, then is he also a mentor? If Enkidu is Gilgamesh's mentor (which seems doubtful), then what is the role of Utnapishtim, the "immortal" man sought by Gilgamesh in order to question him about life and death? I also wonder how Enkidu's sexual awakening and struggle with Gilgamesh relates to Iron John's transformation. Perhaps Humbaba would have been a better example of the "wild man" in ancient literature, and the meaning of the Gilgamesh epic would have been revealed as a tragic confession of the results of killing this untamed forest-dweller who was willing to serve his human conqueror.

The questions raised by *Iron John* need to be addressed if there is to be any hope of individual liberation and cultural freedom. The disappearance of the initiatory process and the devaluation of the role of the mentor (along with a right understanding of what a mentor is and does) in modern society are just now being felt in a new way. We need to face that loss squarely and ask ourselves, What next? What are we to do?

Bly's approach, while no doubt sincere, is perhaps more a reaction than a response to our needs. We must ask whether a broken tradition can be restored, and if so, how? Can the "initiatory process" be reclaimed, or even understood, by those who have not lived it in the traditional sense? Can someone who has never had a mentor take on the role of mentor?

One solution has been suggested by Bly and the "men's movement": *go back*. But can we? As a modern man, I find myself "in between": in between the wish to go back, to restore what has been lost, and the knowledge that the only way truly to arrive at what I seek is by going forward. It will be interesting to track the influence of *Iron John* over the coming years, to see whether it will act as a catalyst for further questioning on issues of gender and liberation, and whether the idea of discipline, which Bly introduces but upon which he does not expand, will be a part of the new discussion. Regardless of the outcome, Bly's richly provocative book is a boon to both men and women who seek to understand themselves and the culture in which they live.

—Stuart Smithers

Stuart Smithers is a professor of religion at the University of Puget Sound.

PARABOLA BOOKS & AUDIO ON NATIVE AMERICAN SPIRITUALITY

1990 Benjamin Franklin Award Winner

I BECOME PART OF IT
Sacred Dimensions in Native American Life

Edited by D.M. Dooling & Paul Jordan-Smith
Introduction by Joe Bruchac

An anthology of compelling articles by Native Americans such as Arthur Amiotte, Vine Deloria, Oren Lyons, and Emory Sekaquaptewa, and Native American scholars Joseph Epes Brown, Sam Gill, Barbara Tedlock, and Barre Toelken, interspersed with traditional Native stories and contemporary art.

". . . welcome relief from the flood of pseudo-Indian spirituality cluttering libraries and bookstores . . . impeccable scholarship and valuable insights."
—Library Journal

"An important and unusually accessible contribution."
—Kirkus

$14.95; 304 pages; softcover; 15 illustrations

THE SONS OF THE WIND
The Sacred Stories of the Lakota

Edited by D.M. Dooling

The mythology of the Oglala Lakota, that historic and still living tribe of the Sioux Nation who are the people of Crazy Horse, Red Cloud, and Black Elk, of Little Big Horn and Wounded Knee. Based on the Walker manuscripts, the stories are presented here for the first time in a continuous narrative form accessible to all lovers of myth and poetry.

"An eloquent and accessible rendering of the mighty creation myth of the Lakota people, which ranks among the most stirring in earth literature."
—Peter Matthiessen

"unfolds like a novel."
—Barry Lopez

$8.95; 168 pages; softcover

NEW FROM THE PARABOLA AUDIO LIBRARY

Storytime Series

THE BOY WHO LIVED WITH THE BEARS AND OTHER IROQUOIS STORIES

Told by Joe Bruchac

This collection of six Native American tales is the first of a new series which offers children of all ages traditional stories told by traditional storytellers.

These six stories, from the Iroquois people, or "Haudenosaunee," which means "People of the Longhouse," are of the adventures and misadventures of rabbit and buzzard, turtle and bear, and of one small boy who is befriended by all the animals of the forest. Between the stories the listener will hear drumming and the spirited "call and response" between the storyteller and his audience.

Joe Bruchac—or *Sozap*, as he is known under his Abenaki name—is a well-known storyteller and writer of Abenaki, English and Slovak ancestry.

"Entertaining, dramatic, intelligent stories told with beautiful simplicity and authority."
— *Ursula K. Le Guin*

Total running time: 63 min. $9.95 ISBN 0-930407-19-9

Please use the order form bound between pages 96 and 97.

Icons and the Mystical Origins of Christianity
By Richard Temple. Shaftesbury, England: Element Books, 1990. Pp. 198. $15.95, paper.

OUR CULTURE has become so separated from its higher origins that, for many of us today, "sacred art" is almost a contradiction in terms: if it is art it cannot be sacred, and if it is sacred it cannot be art.

To begin to draw these two life-sustaining streams together again is an undertaking of major importance, but this task requires both knowledge and experience not commonly found in the West or the East. Ananda Coomaraswamy made a superb beginning two generations ago in relation to South Asian art and tradition. In his own way, Richard Temple has set himself a similar task in relation to Russian and Greek Orthodox art—one for which he is well suited as the founder and moving spirit of the Temple Gallery in London, long known for its fine collections of Eastern Christian art. *Icons and the Mystical Origins of Christianity* is the mature fruit of his search to understand the meaning and true nature of the greatest icons, which call us to a vision of the world and of ourselves from which most of us have been too long separated.

As Jacob Needleman writes in his foreword to the book,

> Sacred art may be defined as art that evokes and supports an inner movement towards contact with a greater reality. But it cannot do this automatically; it requires that we bring something of ourselves to it. . . . These ideas challenge us to think in a new way, not only about Christianity, but about life itself. And to think in a new way is the first step towards that unique event of the human psyche called seeing. Neither ideas nor images alone can cause us to see, but they can orient our intention and guide us towards the act of opening to the universal mystery that has neither name nor form.

So, too, for Temple, "the ultimate encounter with the mysteries of the gospel is not to be sought in historical time but in the present moment." That is the only time when a great icon can speak to me and illuminate my understanding—suddenly and unexpectedly. It is more likely to happen in the mind within the heart than in the head-brain. But in preparation for that moment, it helps to know the background of ideas that the icon masters shared and that Temple shares with us.

Others have written brilliantly about the art history of Orthodox icons and the stylistic developments from St. Catherine's Monastery at Mount Sinai in the sixth century, through the flowering of the Byzantine at the Kariye Djami in Con-

stantinople, to the astonishing Russian masters of the fourteenth and fifteenth centuries. With fifty-six black-and-white photos and illustrations, and one color plate, Temple shows us that he is thoroughly familiar with this material, but it is not his main concern. As we stand with him in front of, for example, Rublyov's Christ Pantocrator, we can be struck by its beauty and power, but also be hungry for clues to what it means. Temple relates to us the ideas and spiritual practices that formed masters like Rublyov, tracing this ancient teaching from its pre-Christian origins in Egypt and Greece (Hermes, Plato, Plotinus), through the Gnostics and Desert Fathers of early Christianity, to the hesychasts of Mount Athos. As Temple shows, the greatest painters of icons were steeped in the esoteric teachings and practices of hesychasm as written down in the Philokalia, a book which few art historians have read, still less put into practice. A mind unfurnished can still be filled with wonder, but unless the heart has been long engaged in what hesychasts called "inner warfare," even the greatest icons can convey to us only a limited sense of awakening and opening to a force or a light which we could truly describe as "higher." To participate fully in the experience which such icons can transmit, we must become fellow pilgrims with the artist, sharing his world view and his struggle towards the light.

Temple's chapter on Light is for me the heart of his book. In it he explains,

> We cannot apprehend reality in our ordinary way of living. The poverty of our spiritual circumstances is such that all our beliefs and values must be regarded as provisional and ultimately of limited validity. Objectively, the only thing of real consequence for man, while on earth, is the possible role for him in the maintenance of cosmic harmony within the order of the universe. God helps man to realise this possibility by sending down to him his Divine Energies. These are symbolized in Christian literature and art as light. He also, in a way incomprehensible to us, sends himself as Christ, the Divine Logos. . . . We see in the icons that Christ is depicted in the attributes of light . . . All religions and philosophies have recognized this; the Buddhists strive for illumination; the Sufi mystics seek enlightenment; Jesus said: 'I am the light of the world.'

Just as that light of the Logos came into the world through the Virgin Mary, so we, looking with open eyes at an icon of the Annunciation or the Nativity, can come to understand that these glowing paintings are not only teaching us about Christ's birth long ago, but are calling us to the birth of the same light in our own hearts now. As Angelus Silesius has said, "I myself must become Mary and give birth to God."

For the rapture of its wild genius, MacKenna's Plotinus has been for near to 40 years **the most instructive and inspiring single volume in my library.** It is a source of the deepest ideas the mind can think; it is also a bible of beauty.

—James Hillman

PLOTINUS: The Enneads

A definitive edition of the classic translation by
STEPHEN MACKENNA

Deep religious feeling, breathtaking beauty, vigor, and lucidity make this simply the most inspired English translation of one of the finest products of the human mind. This new, limited-edition, first quality hardcover shows all significant changes made in revised editions after MacKenna's death, with comparisons to other major translators on key passages. Est. 700 pages , 6 x 9, cloth

PRE-PUBLICATION SPECIAL OFFER
Projected retail price: $65 **Pre-pub price until 9/9/91: $45**
Delivery: late September 1991

SONG AND ITS FOUNTAINS

by A.E.

"For those who would see with a poet's clarity of vision . . . this book offers vistas so endless there is no possibility of getting to their end."

—*New York Times*
April 1932

A catalyzing, poetically beautiful introspection into the *process* of inspired creativity. This back-in-print classic sparkles with the intuitive vision and robust practicality that made this versatile and beloved genius the key figure of the Celtic literary renaissance.

110 pages, paper, $10.95

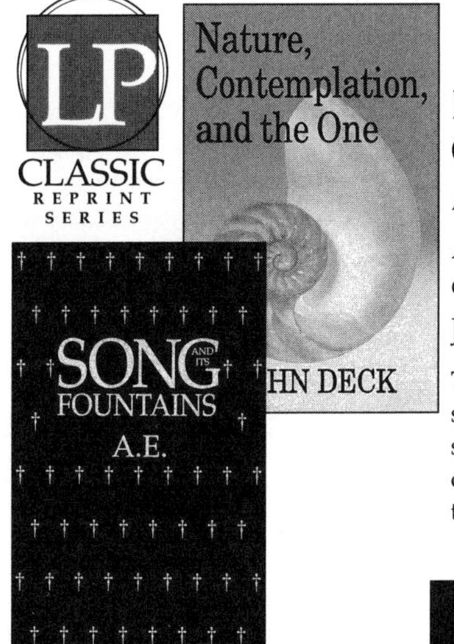

NATURE, CONTEMPLATION, AND THE ONE

A Study in the Philosophy of Plotinus *by*
JOHN DECK

This brilliant, concise study shows how, for Plotinus, the sensible world arises as the contemplative *act* of living, intelligent Mind.

160 pages, paper, $14.95

See Parabola review this issue!

"A truly great man . . . one of my closest spiritual brothers."
—H.H. the Dalai Lama

"A marvelous introduction both to meditation and to epistemology . . . a very 'modern' work." —Christopher Bamford, *Gnosis*

LOOKING INTO MIND

How to Recognize Who You Are and How You Know
by Anthony Damiani
298 pages, paper, $14.95

How to Recognize
LOOKING
Who You Are and
INTO
How You Know
MIND
Anthony
Damiani

TO ORDER with MasterCard or Visa *only*: 1-800-828-2197.
Or, with payment, by mail: Larson Publications, 4936P State Route 414, Burdett, NY 14818. U.S. funds only. Please add $3 shipping for first item, $.50 for each additional.
For more information: 607-546-9342

In concluding, Temple sadly concedes that by the sixteenth century, Western cultural influences had already begun to erode the basis of Orthodox icon painting, bringing in alien styles and values. "Icons exist to convey the highest cosmological, philosophical and theological ideas. They were brought into being and developed a thousand years ago and more in order to provide insight into traditions and scriptures from which grew what we call Christianity. . . . Though the art of icon could not survive [the onslaught of Western influences]," Temple affirms that "the perennial ideas on which it is founded are indestructible."

This is a courageous book, going against the stream of contemporary opinions holding that art and the sacred are, and should be, separate. By showing how intimately they can be related, he gives us an invaluable lesson that can be applied not only to Orthodox Christianity but to all the great traditions for whom art and the sacred have always been joined.

—*James George*

In the course of his career as a Canadian diplomat, James George has studied icons in many countries of the Near and Middle East.

The Hebrew Goddess

By Raphael Patai. Third enlarged edition. Detroit: Wayne State University Press, 1990. Pp. 368. $35.00, cloth; $16.00, paper.

THE MAIN THESIS of Raphael Patai's *The Hebrew Goddess*, first published in 1967 and now appearing in a new and expanded edition, is as arresting as its title. Throughout history, the author claims,

Jews have worshiped a female goddess in addition to YHWH, the fierce but loving male God of the Hebrew Bible. In extraordinarily lucid and lively language, Patai arrays the evidence for his provocative assertion, focusing on developments in the Biblical, Talmudic, and medieval periods.

Citing numerous verses from the Bible, the author easily demonstrates that worship of Asherah, a Canaanite goddess, was prevalent among the ancient Hebrews, as was worship of Ba'al, a Canaanite god. A statue of Asherah was erected in the first Jerusalem Temple, remained there for many centuries, and most likely played a part in the official cult. Even more remarkable, he notes, is that Asherah worship did not trouble the great reformer and prophets as much as Ba'al worship did. When Elijah slaughtered the 450 priests of Ba'al after the dramatic confrontation on Mount Carmel, he left the 400 priests of Asherah unharmed. This goddess' continued grip on the people, according to Patai, reflects their deep-seated psychological need for a fertility-bestowing mother goddess.

One of the most fascinating chapters in the first part of this volume deals with the cherubs, the winged human forms that perched on both sides of the ark in the Holy of Holies. These cherubs have long been a thorn in the side of Jewish thinkers who find themselves at a loss to explain how a strictly monotheistic religion could prescribe that two "idols" be placed in God's holiest chamber. Patai, citing descriptions of icons in the ancient world and also several passages from the Talmud, concludes that the cherubs did not assume the shape of young boys but of a male and female locked in marital embrace. This, he claims, provides additional evidence of the staying power of goddess worship in ancient Israel.

In the Talmudic period (200 B.C.-700 A.D.) goddess worship was largely suppressed. The only significant development is the appearance of a new name for God, Shekhinah, first introduced by the Bible translator Onkelos to represent that aspect of God that the human senses are able to apprehend.

With the emergence of Jewish mysticism in the Middle Ages, goddess worship returned to the fore. Although the mystics continued to see God as one, at the same time they viewed him as a series of ten emanations, the lowest of which they called Shekhinah, a feminine noun denoting God's feminine principle. As long as the temple stood, so says the basic mystical myth, God was able to consort with his female side in his sacred place. But with the destruction of the temple and the ensuing exile, the two became separated. From that time on,

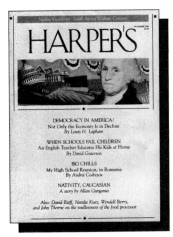

the mission of Jews the world over is to bring about the reunification of the divine couple.

One way of accomplishing this goal is the frequent uttering of mystical incantations, known as *yihudim* (literally, unifications). In one of the new chapters in this edition of *The Hebrew Goddess*, Patai presents a detailed discussion of the development and rapid spread of these prayers. Despite the adamant rabbinic opposition to their inclusion in the *siddur* (prayerbook), an indication of the educated elite's rejection of the female aspect of the Godhead, these prayers found their way in. Their enduring popularity, even in modern times, is proof, according to the author, that belief in the Shekhinah and its reunification with God is "a living part of the belief system" of many Jewish communities today.

As engaging, wide-ranging, and thought-provoking as Patai's volume is, I have reservations about his less-than-rigorous research methods. In the chapter on Lilith, the she-demon who is depicted as the first wife of Adam, Patai's evidence does not warrant the conclusion that she is a product of the Talmudic mind. Upon consulting the notes, I discovered that the long story he recounts about her is drawn not from a Talmudic but a post-Talmudic source. Furthermore, although the Talmud refers to a whole class of demons called liliths, nowhere does it use Lilith as a proper name. This implies that the fully developed character of Lilith is not a product of rabbinic theology but medieval mysticism.

Another methodological reservation is that Patai amply cites sources that support his thesis but fails to address those that do not. When arguing that the cherubs according to the Talmud were male and female, he does not tell the reader about the other passages that consider them to be young boys. Nor does he satisfactorily explain why he favors pronouncements by Talmudic rabbis living at least two hundred years after the destruction of the temple over two contemporary descriptions, one by Philo and the other by Josephus, which do not note the presence of a female cherub.

Finally, Patai overstates his case about the widespread belief in the Shekhinah today as suggested by the popularity of the unification utterances. He himself quotes a rabbi who says that 99 per cent of the people do not know what these prayers mean. More importantly, the *yihudim* are viewed by many—who come to understand them in English translation—not as a mystical incantation but as a useful strategy for concentrating on the prayer about to be recited or the action about to be performed.

Despite my many reservations, Patai has convinced me of two major parts of his thesis: that in the Biblical period many Jews, ignoring the dire warnings of the prophets, worshiped a goddess along with God; and that with the flourishing of mysticism in the medieval period, there is a resurgence of interest in the feminine principle of God. That these two facts are intimately related to each other and that in the intervening years there were rumblings of goddess worship, I find hard to accept.

—Judith Hauptman

Judith Hauptman is associate professor of Talmud at the Jewish Theological Seminary.

Looking Into Mind

By Anthony Damiani. Burdett, NY: Larson Publications, 1990. Pp. *xv* + 282. $14.95, paper.

IN HIS *Of the Principles of Human Knowledge* (1710), Bishop Berkeley argues that "bodies which

compose the mighty frame of the world, have not any subsistence without a mind, that their *being* is to be perceived or known." Substance, materiality, solidity, weight, extension, and resistance—all the ways we qualify experiences with bodies—are, therefore, ideas or thought-constructs. They exist only in the mind. Berkeley goes on to conclude, "There is not any other substance than *spirit*, or that which perceives."

This idealist or "mentalist" position, moreover, is not confined to Western thought. Berkeley presents his *esse est percipi* in opposition to John Locke's realism, which holds that material bodies really exist. Analogously, the Yogacarin school of Buddhism attacks Madhyamika for holding a similar belief and argues the sole reality is of consciousness (*vijnana*): the external world and all our assumptions about it are unfounded and empty of substance.

This background is helpful in understanding the prime intention of Anthony Damiani's book: to undermine naive realism. Viewing things as external to ourselves, we react with domination, manipulation, and violence. Our drive to achievement is based on the premise that the world exists independently and is over and against ourselves. Damiani argues persuasively that when the root cause of projection—the attitude that physical bodies exist independent of our ideas—is cut, the flower of delusion will wither.

Since Berkeley's (and the Yogacarin's) argument today lies forgotten, Damiani has performed an important service. As a leading student of Paul Brunton, he explicates difficult passages in Brunton's texts. Brunton writes that "every presented thing which is seen, smelled, heard, felt, or tasted, no less than every representative thought, idea, name, or image, is entirely mental." If a difficulty arises in comprehending this philosophical position, a considerably greater one awaits the attempt to experience its living truth. "Mentalism teaches a view of physical existence which seems to contradict every experience of daily living," according to Brunton. One must come to see the habitual, almost instantaneous interpretation—mistaken for reality—by which moment by moment we engender the external world. As Brunton puts it, "The existence of the world is not a testimony to the existence of a divine creator, but to the constructive capacity of the mind."

This work by Damiani is roughly divided between theoretical exegesis and practical suggestion. The text itself is a transcription of discussions given over a ten-day period in Sweden in 1983. His language is informal, direct, sometimes confrontational. Responses are replete with personal anecdotes, asides, teaching tales, and philosophical ramblings. Themes appear, disappear, and get repeated and entangled. The form is both strength and weakness. The reader is witness to the give-and-take of vitalizing conversation but at the same time misses the more fully developed thought of the solitary moment. Though further editing and consolidation might have eliminated these deficiencies, when nuggets appear, their value is immediately felt. That so much depends on the weight of the question to which Damiani responds reminds one of the debt that a guide owes to the perplexed.

Damiani urges us to "be concerned with 'how' rather than 'why'—because 'whys' are forever. The 'how' is what you want to know." He himself is, however, most convincing with explanations and proofs of the constructive tendencies of ordinary mind. David Hume, Buddhism, and quantum physics all point to mentalism's truth. "Because if you analyze an object . . . , you'll come up like the modern scientist and say there's no substantial thing there, there's only whirling protonic and electronic energies, there's nothing there, no *thing* is there."

Between intellectual deduction and embodied knowledge yawns a great gulf. How does one verify for oneself the repeated capture of attention by the ordinary mind's ready conceptual scheme? How does one acknowledge the loss of freedom and vision when focused on the objective world? The clues Damiani offers—those of a longtime practitioner—provide insight if one is willing to make the payment. He urges sensitivity to a new quality of life. As Brunton writes, "Once you have caught this inner note in your experience of your own self-existence, try to adhere firmly to the listening attitude which catches it." Or: "At the centre of each man, each animal, each plant, each cell, and each atom, there is a complete stillness. A seemingly empty stillness, yet it holds the divine energies and the divine Idea for that thing."

Also urged is the ability to follow thought. The ordinary, projective mind "is like a grasshopper." We require a finer attention and a new mind in order to allow another quality of thinking to become incarnate. When the thought that objectifies is stilled, we come to the self-contained clarity of the mind that does not "go out." Through it, testimony about our place and our purpose can become manifest. Furthermore, the new non-projective mind is not a replacement for our ordinary one. It is rather a matter of relation and right function. As Damiani puts it, "The goal, the ideal should not be to obliterate the thinking mind. The goal should be to develop and fulfill the thinking mind."

—David Appelbaum

David Appelbaum is a professor of philosophy at SUNY New Paltz, and the coeditor of Real Philosophy *(Penguin).*

The Myth of Shangri-la: Tibet, Travel Writing and the Western Creation of Sacred Landscape
By Peter Bishop. Berkeley: University of California Press, 1989. Pp. 308. $29.95, cloth.

A History of Modern Tibet 1913-1951: The Demise of the Lamaist State
By Melvyn Goldstein. Berkeley: University of California Press, 1989. Pp. 898. $85.00, cloth.

THESE ARE TWO important studies of Tibet, but important in quite different ways. One describes the Tibet that the West has created over the last two centuries, the white peaks of the Land of Snows providing the ultimate screen for the projection of a wide range of fantasies, some benighted, some benign. The other is a monumental account of the byzantine world of Tibetan politics during the first decades of this century, an account that succeeds like no work before it in demolishing our myths of Shangri-la.

Peter Bishop's *The Myth of Shangri-la* sets out to be something other than a narrative account of nineteenth- and twentieth-century British travel writing about Tibet. British travelogues certainly provide his data, but his task is to explore representations of Tibet in this literature, illustrating how a rather motley crew of explorers, soldiers, spies, eccentrics, and mystics found in the landscape of Tibet, both near and from afar, the fulfillment of their fantasies of the mysterious Other. Some were repulsed, others captivated, but for all, Tibet held a particular fascination as the most remote of destinations, ruled by the enigmatic Dalai Lama in the holy city of Lhasa. Tibet exercised a peculiar hold on the colonial mentality precisely because it was never a colony, and thus has remained a pristine subject of romantic musings until the present day. Bishop has done an admirable job of combing through massive amounts of literature to produce his analysis, rich with citation and theoretically informed by such diverse thinkers as Jung, Said, James Hillman, and Foucault.

Goldstein's *A History of Modern Tibet 1913-1951* is, simply stated, the most important book on Tibetan history yet produced in the West. It is a straightforward and sober narrative of the thirty-nine years of this century during which Tibet held complete control over both its internal and foreign affairs. In 1913, the thirteenth Dalai Lama returned from exile in India to expel all Chinese officials from Tibet. In 1951, a delegation of officials of the government of the fourteenth Dalai Lama signed in Peking (some say under duress) the Seventeen Point Agreement which ceded much of Tibet's political autonomy to the People's Republic of China. The signal value of Goldstein's history is that it is based largely on in-depth interviews with the participants, the surviving cabinet ministers, local officials, and bureaucrats of the old Tibetan government, now living in exile in India and the West. With the invaluable aid of Ngawang Gelek Rimpoche, Goldstein was able to elicit candid accounts of the pivotal events of Tibetan history during the twentieth century, free from the sanitizing that has often distorted our view of Tibet in the past.

NEW

LYRICO

The Only Horse of His Kind

by Elizabeth Vincent Foster
Illustrations by Joy Buba

"In the constant stream of books for children, all too often of one type and one general tone, LYRICO stands out like a shining lump of pure gold in a streambed of gravel."

—DEIRDRE LAROUCHE, ST. LOUIS POST-DISPATCH

A delightful blend of fantasy and natural history, *Lyrico* is a modern allegory about a young girl and a flying horse. Elizabeth Foster's text and Joy Buba's illustrations gently call the young reader to question the values of materialistic society.

This is a story of Philippa, who has everything that money can buy, but who still longs for something more in her life. Then she is given a marvelous gift by the mysterious Mr. Olympio—a tiny silvery grey horse with wings. Together they learn to fly high above the skyscrapers of the city until Lyrico's need for the air and freedom of the mountains lead them on a perilous journey westward, to Myth Valley.

This is Elizabeth Foster's first novel, one which she undertook in collaboration with her long-time friend, Joy Buba. The two enjoy a shared love of horses which has taken them on several pack trips into the mountains of northern Montana. The resulting volume of text and drawings is a blend of their enthusiasm for the wildlife of the mountains and a lively interest in mythology and story.

"She would look down into the valley, thousands of feet below, with Myth Creek a blue thread squiggling in the bottom of it, and at the snow-streaked crags of the opposite mountains, and up at the precipice of Myth Peak towering above her, and at the precious dainty plants, like fairies' flower-beds, brightening the bare rock beside her—and would wonder if anybody, anywhere had ever felt so happy."

ISBN 0-930407-21-0
230 pages, paperback; 50 black & white illustrations $10.95

Please use the order form bound between pages 96 and 97.

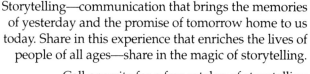

Goldstein's account reads like a novel; for the student of Tibet it is impossible to set down, despite its considerable bulk. He provides the most detailed description to date of the so-called Reting affair, which precipitated a revolt by the monks of Che College of Sera Monastery that was only ended when the Tibetan army moved artillery into position below Sera and began shelling the monastery. This occurred in April of 1947, when the present Dalai Lama was eleven years old.

In addition to recounting the intrigues of Tibetan palace politics, Goldstein's history provides the most detailed and accurate account of the last days before the Chinese invasion of 1950, of the Tibetans' doomed attempts to find a sympathetic ear in London and Washington, and of the Dalai Lama's negotiations with Mao in Peking.

Goldstein's history clearly shows that, at least in the first decades of this century, the government of Tibet was corrupt, with excessive power concentrated in the hands of the conservative abbots of the great monasteries of Lhasa and he demonstrates that the Dalai Lama, even the progressive thirteenth, in the final analysis had very little power.

We might pause to consider why we find Goldstein's account so devastating. Why is it disillusioning to learn that large segments of the monastic population had few concerns beyond the acquisition of wealth and power, when such concerns are so familiar to us from our own ecclesiastical history? It is perhaps because the myth of Tibet, as a haven beyond a world obsessed with politics and power, is so strong that our investment in the fantasy (aptly described in Bishop's book) is so compelling. The participation in the fantasy of Tibet is not entirely neurotic so far as it serves our ability to imagine an ideal. But the fantasy does a great disservice to the real Tibet and the real Tibetans, whom we will find ever lacking for their failure to fulfill our romantic illusions. Such a disservice is especially dangerous at the present time when Tibet most desperately needs our clear and unambiguous support in its efforts to resist Chinese colonization. Goldstein and Bishop have provided us with the tools to demythologize Tibet, if not entirely to dispel our myths, then at least to allow us to see them for what they are. It is only when such disillusionment has taken place that we can truly begin to understand Tibet and its extraordinary culture.

—*Donald S. Lopez, Jr.*

Donald S. Lopez, Jr. is Professor of Buddhist and Tibetan Studies at the University of Michigan.

Ludwig Wittgenstein: The Duty of Genius

By Ray Monk. New York: The Free Press, 1990. Pp. *xviii* + 654. $29.95, cloth. Illustrated.

LUDWIG WITTGENSTEIN, who died in 1951, remains a figure of fascination eighty years after he first burst onto the intellectual scene, descending on Cambridge to become Bertrand Russell's protégé and soon his hectoring master. He is doubtless the dominant force in twentieth-century philosophy. Anyone who studies philosophy has to deal with him, since his teaching transformed the field into linguistic analysis, despite his railing against the academic incarceration of the philosophic quest. For perhaps millions, he is philosophy incarnate, though few—even professional philosophers—know much about him or his real aims. To most intellectual "tourists" (as he called those who lack total dedication), he is simply a manic professor who made philosophy into a forbidding stew of endless analysis and mystification. But he embodies as well, at least unconsciously, the archetype of the ruthless pursuer of truth. It is Wittgenstein's love for truth that ultimately fuels not only an industry of commentaries and elaborations, but novels, art, theology, and Woody Allen jokes.

Wittgenstein's life is a biographer's dream and nightmare. His story brims with outer and inner drama. He was born in Vienna in 1889 (the same year as Hitler, who attended the same school), the eighth and last child of Karl Wittgenstein, one of the richest, most powerful men of his day, and his wife Leopoldine, who shared with Ludwig her love of music. Ludwig grew up in the Palais Wittgenstein, thrust into a mostly tragic play loaded with paternal dictates, prodigal sons, remote mothering, and the hubbub of an ever-changing supporting cast of servants and tutors, industrialists and artists. The period was *fin de siècle*, the atmosphere a mix of opulence and despair. Beneath its "nervous splendor," Wittgenstein's Vienna was the birthplace of Nazism and Zionism, Russian Communism and psychoanalysis. His three oldest brothers committed suicide (the all-or-nothing temptation that also plagued him), and his brother Paul, who lost an arm in the war, drove himself to become a one-handed

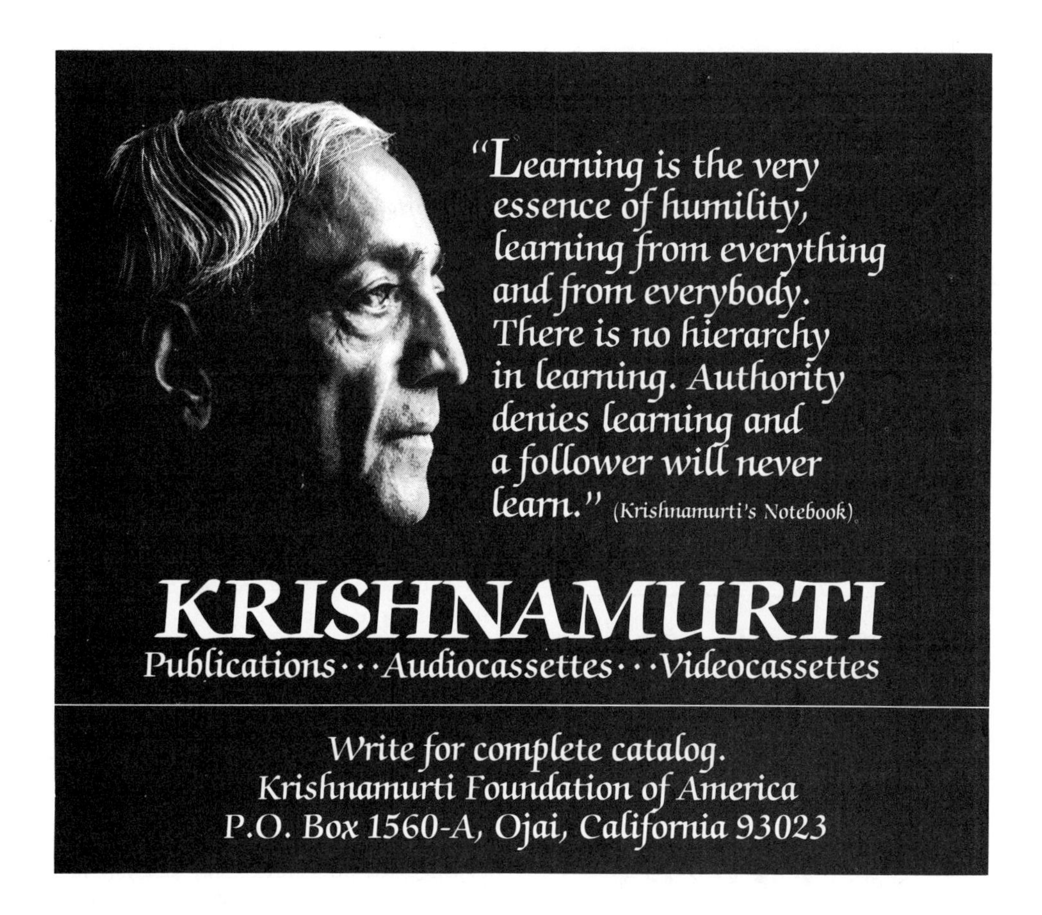

piano virtuoso (for whom Ravel wrote his *Concerto for the Left Hand*).

Cowed but watchful, Wittgenstein didn't talk until he was four, dithered at school, sought to please and to avoid his brothers' self-destructive rebellions, and pursued an engineering career he knew his father would approve. It was the mathematical theory underlying engineering that opened up his philosophical vocation. At Cambridge, his eccentric brilliance quickly brought him within the circle of G.E. Moore, the self-effacing guru of the "Apostles," the infamous conversation society that embraced both Bloomsbury (Lytton Strachey, Leonard Woolf, John Maynard Keynes, *et al.*) and later the Kim Philby and Anthony Blunt spy ring.

While serving with gloomy valor in the Austrian army in World War I, Wittgenstein not only completed his landmark *Tractatus Logico-Philosophicus*, whose laconic pronouncements he thought settled all the crucial questions of philosophy, but underwent a radical conversion to a Tolstoyan Christianity that led him to renounce all his wealth when he returned to Vienna as one of the richest men in Europe. He then labored as a monastic gardener, a rural school teacher, and an architect. Later he returned to philosophy through agonized encounters with the Vienna Circle, who reduced truth to what could be scientifically verified, and eventually through embattled stints at Cambridge, where he became a walking legend, mesmerizing colleagues and students who went on to institutionalize his legacy. He escaped Cambridge as often as he could to devote himself—in a remote cabin in Norway, the woodsman's hut on his family's country estate, a hotel room in Dublin, a cottage on the Irish coast—to formulating his ideas.

Throughout his life, Wittgenstein was racked by doubts about his integrity and his work. He depended on the emotional and practical support of people like Russell, Moore, and Keynes, but was brutally honest, devastatingly critical, and utterly dismissive when they didn't measure up to his expectations. "Well, God has arrived. I met him on the 5.15 train," Keynes once announced to his wife. He craved the friendship of bright, kind, attentive, above all *serious* young men (occasionally women), but even the three men and one woman with whom he fell deeply in love found him generous yet demanding, devoted yet allergic to intimacy.

Ray Monk's account is a remarkable accomplishment on at least two counts. He is the first to piece together all the salient details of a life that both Wittgenstein and his literary heirs seemed determined to leave in obscurity so that only the work would survive for scrutiny. More, he has discerned the driving spirit of the man, revealing that his purpose was to demonstrate the limits of language and scientific rationality so as to disclose the true, crucial realm of religion and morality, which can be lived but not explained.

The vital features of Wittgenstein's life yield a compelling picture when he is seen as a distinctly modern kind of saint, albeit a holy terror. "I would (often) rather have a happy *person* for a brother than an unhappy *saint*," his sister Hermine lamented. Like other absolutist Austrians, he had a consuming passion for getting things right. He realized that the only way to begin to straighten out society was to eliminate the deceptions of our language and hence our thinking, and that meant primarily to free oneself of illusions. He was absolute in his pursuit of perfection in himself, in his work, and in others. When one exasperated friend asked, "You want to be perfect?" he roared, "*Of course* I want to be perfect." Asked the meaning of life, he said that all he was sure of was that we are not here "to have a good time."

A monk of the mind, Wittgenstein was a living paradox: a Jew raised a Catholic; equally obsessed by "logic and his sins"; a cultured Austrian stuck amid British life he found shallow and false; an aristocrat who lived in stark simplicity; a logician on a mystical quest; a homosexual who despised gay life; a professor who found the university "a living death." At the end of a life riddled with angst, his final words were "Tell them I've had a wonderful life."

Ray Monk's achievement is not without shortcomings. The book, with its Britishisms, foreign phrases, patches of calculus, is tailored to those who share his Oxbridgean education and won't be easily caught in the thickets of technical philosophizing (which do give a taste of Wittgenstein's own labyrinthine lectures). More significantly, Monk—to use a Wittgensteinian distinction—*says* more than he *shows* about what made his subject unique: rarely does the reader experience the intense atmosphere in which Wittgenstein lived, his magnetism and terror, his titanic inner struggles. And he may not take seriously enough Wittgenstein's Catholic background, which however superficial and rejected, seems an obvious source of his obsession with perfection, acute sense of sin, judgment, and damnation, his Augustinian need to confess, his emphasis on doing and life of attempted chastity, poverty, and his obedience to his calling. Despite his protests, he seems a very Catholic Jew, this pilgrim who didn't believe enough to become a priest, but spent all his energy striving to save his and others' souls.

Still, these cavils ought not to gainsay the fact that Monk's work reveals far more about the vital interplay of Wittgenstein's life and thought than any book to date.

For me, Wittgenstein's life raises two questions: How is it possible to live seriously, to be dedicated to the highest standards, without becoming "an impossible person" (as one no-nonsense teenager dubbed him)? And can one be truly religious in the sense of seeking only the best in oneself and others, without becoming engaged with traditional religious teaching—is there a post-traditional religious way? Wittgenstein evokes, in Iris Murdoch's words, "awe and alarm," leaving one to wonder how his quest can be fulfilled in a more joyous human life.

—John Loudon

John Loudon, senior editor of HarperSanFrancisco, is writing a dramatic life of Wittgenstein.

CREDITS

Cover The Shoemaker. From Jost Amman and Hans Sachs, *The Book of Trades* (New York: Dover Publications, Inc., 1973).

Page 4 Relief with chisel and mallet. From Kurt Weitzmann, ed., *Age of Spirituality* (New York: Metropolitan Museum of Art, 1979).

Page 5 Carpenters at work. Miniature from the Bible of King Venceslas. From Václav Husa, with Josef Petráň and Alena Šubrtová, *Hommes et Métiers* (Paris: Librairie Gründ, 1967).

Pages 6 - 8 "The Coppersmith" (p. 6); "The Book Printer" (p. 7); "The Bell Maker (p. 8). From Jost Amman and Hans Sachs, *The Book of Trades* (New York: Dover Publications, Inc., 1973).

Pages 11 - 13 Arachne as spider (p. 11); Arachne and Athene weaving (p.13). From Ingri and Edgar Parin D'Aulaire, *Book of Greek Myths* (New York: Doubleday, 1962).

Pages 14 - 22 Photographs © 1991 by Lee B. Ewing.

Page 24 Penelope, Odysseus, and the suitors. Illustration by Pauline Baynes. From Roger Lancelyn Green, *The Tale of Troy: Retold from the Ancient Authors* (London: Penguin Books, 1974).

Page 26 Calligrapher at work. Illustration from a 16th-century Turkish manuscript of 'Ajā'ib al-Makhlūqāt ('The Wonders of Creation') by al-Qazwīnī. From Yasin Hamid Safadi, *Islamic Calligraphy* (London: Thames and Hudson, 1978).

Page 27 Page from the Koran in a type of Kufic script. Persia, 11th century. *Ibid.*

Page 29 Zoomorphic calligraphy, Shī'ah prayer in Thuluth in the shape of a falcon. Persia, early 19th century. *Ibid.*

Pages 30 - 31 Initial letter 'M' (p. 30); initial letter 'G' (p. 31). From *Victor Hammer: Artist and Printer* (Lexington: Anvil Press, 1981).

Page 32 Specimen of 18 pt. American Uncial.

Page 34 Initial letter 'E.' From *Victor Hammer: Artist and Printer* (Lexington: Anvil Press, 1981).

Page 35 Initial letter in Victor Hammer's *Memory and Her Nine Daughters, the Muses* (Lexington: Stamperia del Santuccio, 1956).

Page 37 Brok at the furnace with gadfly. Illustration by Willy Pogany. From Padraic Colum, *The Children of Odin: The Book of Northern Myths* (New York: The Macmillan Company, 1962).

Page 38 One of the dwarfs. Illustration by Arthur Rackham. From Richard Wagner, *The Rhinegold and the Valkyrie* (New York: Garden City Publishing Co., Inc., 1939).

Page 41 Blacksmith working at his forge, 1973. From Patrick R. McNaughton, *The Mande Blacksmiths: Knowledge, Power, and Art in West Africa* (Bloomington and Indianapolis: Indiana University Press, 1988).

Pages 42 and 45 Potter at work (p. 42); Dogon potter (p. 45). From Alain Gallay with Claudine Sauvain-Dugerdil, *Le Sarnyere Dogon: Archéologie d'un Isolat, Mali* (Paris: Éditions ADPF, 1981).

Pages 46 - 49 Illustrations © 1991 by Gladys Remde.

Pages 50 - 57 Photographs © 1991 by Paul Caponigro. All rights reserved. Spiral Motif, End Chamber, Newgrange Tumulus, County Meath, Ireland, 1967 (p. 50); St. Mac Dara's Church, County Galway, Ireland, 1989 (p. 51); St. Cronan Church, County Clare, Ireland, 1989 (p. 53); Reefert Church, Glendalough, Ireland, 1967 (p. 55); Tournous Abbey, France, 1987 (p. 57).

Pages 58 - 66 Photographs © 1991 by Lee B.Ewing.

Page 69 Sculptor working with a flat carving chisel. From Louis Slobodkin, *Sculpture: Principles and Practice* (New York: Dover Publications, Inc., 1949).

Page 70 Cobbler. Fourteenth-century church fresco, Central Bohemia, Czechoslovakia. From Václav Husa, Josef Petráň, and Alena Šubrtová, *op. cit.*

Page 73 Emblem of crossed hammers. *Ibid.*

Page 76 Indian kite. Collection of Ilonka Karasz. From *Design Forecast, No. 1* (Pittsburgh, Pa.: Aluminum Company of America, 1959).

Page 79 Harry Remde's band saw. Photograph © 1991 by Michael Provost.

Page 81 The Hose-maker. Illustration ©. 1991 by Barbara Garrison.

Page 82 A centerman at the 1990 Jump Dance with the vikapuhich basket, beads, woodpecker headband and eagle feather plume. Photograph © 1990 by Chris Peters.

Page 84 A young dancer at the 1990 Pekwon Jump Dance holding the vikapuhich basket aloft. Photograph © 1990 by Chris Peters.

Pages 86 - 87 Indian marionettes. From Bil Baird, *The Art of the Puppet* (New York: Bonanza Books, 1973).

Pages 89 - 90 "The Call (Future Quest)" (p. 89) and "Lesson/Explorer's Procession" (p. 90) from Meredith Monk's *Atlas: an opera in three parts.* Photographs by Jim Caldwell, courtesy of the Houston Grand Opera.

Page 93 The Archangel Gabriel. From a 16th-century Iranian manuscript. Museum of Fine Arts, Boston.

Page 128 Radiograph of the shell of the chambered nautilus. From H.E. Huntley, *The Divine Proportion* (New York: Dover Publications, Inc., 1970).

PROFILES

PAUL CAPONIGRO, one of America's foremost photographers, has taught and conducted private workshops since 1960. He has devoted many years to the study of the craft of printmaking. His love for stone guides his current work of photographing the early churches of Ireland and the Cistercian abbeys of France.

ANANDA K. COOMARASWAMY (1877-1947), art historian, was a key figure in the twentieth-century cultural meeting of East and West. Among his better-known writings are *Christian and Oriental Philosophy of Art, The Transformation of Nature in Art* and *Buddha and the Gospel of Buddhism.*

MARCEL GRIAULE (d. 1956), French anthropologist and ethnologist, directed field studies in Africa from 1928 to 1956. His investigations were documented in over 170 publications including *The Pale Fox* and *Conversations with Ogotemmêli.*

VICTOR HAMMER (1882-1967), Austrian-born painter and friend of Thomas Merton, was a prolific and capable craftsman in various media, including metal engraving, bookbinding, calligraphy, and typography.

JULIAN LANG, of the Karuk tribe, is a tribal scholar, ceremonialist, author, and artist. Currently he serves as research assistant at the Center for Indian Community Development at Humboldt State University in Arcata, California.

GLADYS AND HARRY REMDE, potter and cabinetmaker, live in a large carriage house in New Jersey where they have their workshops.

JEAN SULZBERGER, a senior editor of PARABOLA, has traveled extensively in the Middle East and Central Asia.

THE GOLDEN MEAN

The Next Issue of

PARABOLA

The Magazine of Myth and Tradition

Forthcoming themes will include:
SOLITUDE AND COMMUNITY, LABYRINTH, and
THE ORAL TRADITION.

(For editorial guidelines, write to The Editors, PARABOLA, *369 Ashford Avenue, Dobbs Ferry, N.Y. 10522.)*